"I wish I had had this book when I began theologians' to the reflective task of thinki~~ng about their own theology~~, humility, Colin Harris writes a sophisticated yet accessible primer on the process of theological construction. He wisely understands that humans are relentlessly theological, and his thinking calls us to a more disciplined approach to interpreting our lives in a communal and dynamic way. I recommend this for both classroom and congregational settings."

—*Molly Marshall, President, United Theological Seminary*

"Colin Harris' readable new book reminds me of the four gospels. Like the Gospels, his book is overflowing with parables that are delightful as well as insightful, and it offers an understanding of faith as living in a covenantal relationship with God. Harris is writing especially to Christians who appreciate the religion of their childhood but who, as they read the Bible and as they experience life, find themselves on a journey toward a more mature and consistent understanding of their faith. This book is a manual of wisdom for that journey. It is a gentle wisdom, modest, compassionate, and intensely biblical. I am especially drawn to Harris' highly original suggestion that theology is a pilgrimage toward community."

—*Fisher Humphreys, Professor of Divinity Emeritus, Samford University*

"Colin Harris, in his book, *Keys for Everyday Theologians*, has done what he, an experienced teacher, does best. He has laid out principles of theological study for 'inquiring minds who want to know more.' Far from the perspective of a 'stuffy' academic theologian, his goal as both teacher and author is to help students/readers broaden and deepen their understanding of the religious dimension of their lives to help them be better equipped to deal with life's challenges. Casting the faith as a 'covenantal relationship,' his 'keys' are accompanied by pertinent, easy-to-understand examples of what they mean and how to use them. Understanding that the lens through which we all see issues of faith is unique to our own perspectives, always giving us an incomplete view, this book is a valuable resource for any Bible or faith student who wants to develop more effective ways of reading, studying, and applying scripture to their lives."

—*Clarissa Strickland, Retired Manager of Reference and Referral, Cooperative Baptist Fellowship*

"Colin Harris has not only taught religious studies in college classrooms for 50 years, but he has also been a Sunday school teacher for most of that time. His passion for helping people from all walks of life to develop a working understanding of what one's faith means and how it is lived in real time is matched by his ability to express his thoughts and ideas in ways that everyone comprehends. What Dr. Harris has done for students in his classes, he has also done for everyone who reads *Keys for Everyday Theologians*. Basic concepts, perspectives, and discernments are clearly explained and illustrated, enabling each reader to give voice to their experiences with God and to share the implications of this covenantal relationship with others. The keys identified in this book will provide a framework for dealing with the challenges, questions, and opportunities that emerge from the faith journey so that every pilgrim can become a theologian. I highly recommend *Keys for Everyday Theologians* to all seeking to understand faith in a healthy way and to discuss what is learned in a helpful way."

—*Bob Browning, Retired Pastor*

"In a style that is engaging and informative, Colin Harris invites readers on a journey toward faith and understanding. Doubt and questions are not viewed as a threat to the Christian life, but rather serve as catalysts on this sacred pilgrimage. In a world filled with empty answers and shallow faith, Harris offers a healthy and helpful new perspective, advocating for a belief that is emerging and evolving, growing deeper and wider through thoughtful reflection. He explores not what to believe, but why and how to believe in the postmodern world."

—*Chris George, Senior Pastor, Smoke Rise Baptist Church, Stone Mountain, Ga.*

"As an academic theologian and a fellow pilgrim of faith, Colin Harris embodies what his writing advocates: theology is a life-long process of refining, changing, and growing. He writes for a 'community of everyday theologians on a pilgrimage together,' and this book confirms that he is a faithful guide along the way. This fine work reminds the reader that theology as a shared journey is more about formation than information. It is a grace, a gift, for Harris to invite us along as fellow pilgrims, finding home and hospitality with one another."

—*C. Gregory DeLoach, Dean, McAfee School of Theology, Mercer University*

"Colin Harris begins *Keys for Everyday Theologians* with the statement that every person of faith is a theologian, thus inviting all into the conversation he undertakes in this masterfully crafted work. Part 1 offers keys to unlocking ten basic concepts that shape an individual's theology, and Part 2 addresses many of the specific questions people often ask about their faith. Harris' work reminds us that faith is a life-long pilgrimage, not a destination to which we can arrive and simply 'settle in.' *Keys for Everyday Theologians*, an excellent resource for those with questions about faith in general and for new and 'seasoned' Christians, is ideal for individual reading, Bible study groups, and the seminary classroom."

—*Nancy L. deClaissé-Walford, Carolyn Ward Professor of Old Testament and Biblical Languages,*
McAfee School of Theology, Mercer University

"What you are about to read is a thoughtful and carefully written introduction to important questions that arise almost inevitably from serious reflection upon one's personal faith experience. It comes from the pen of a man who speaks directly to issues and concerns that reflect honest efforts to speak of one's faith intelligibly and convincingly. From his own experience as both student and teacher, Colin carefully and thoughtfully provides for the reader 'keys' to help unlock and understand the perennial dimensions and dynamics of 'faith seeking understanding.' What is theology and how does it relate to faith? How does one's faith find expression in beliefs? Why should one be concerned about intellectual and theological humility? What does honesty have to do with theology? How do the Bible and church tradition relate to personal experience? What constitutes a 'healthy' religion? What is meant by different levels of truth? How does faith relate to science? What is the relationship between faith and history? What does faith have to do with personal development? How does 'my' faith relate to other faiths? And the questions go on and on and on."

—*Duane Davis, Professor Emeritus of Religion and Philosophy, Mercer University*

Keys for
Everyday Theologians

Unlocking the Doors for "Faith Seeking Understanding"

Colin Harris

© 2022
Published in the United States by Nurturing Faith Inc., Macon GA,
www.nurturingfaith.net.

Library of Congress Cataloging-in-Publication Data is available.

ISBN: 978-1-63528-179-8
All rights reserved. Printed in the United States of America

Contents

Introduction

A Theologian? Who Me?

People of faith sometimes hesitate at the suggestion that they are by definition "theologians." The word tends to conjure up an image of an ordained church leader or an academic professional with formal training in the field. And, to be sure, such persons have carried the discipline of theology in a formal way through the generations, providing a structure and basis for the church's understanding of its faith.

Also, the accumulated work of formal theologians is massive to the point of being overwhelming to many people who attempt to delve into it. Its complexity can easily dissuade those with casual interest and even those required to study it.

But there is another level of theological thinking that goes on in the life and mind of every adherent to a faith. It usually does not lead to formal expression in a systematic way, but it becomes the working understanding of what one's faith means and how it is lived in real time. It is to this kind of theological thinking and to those who engage in it that I offer this "set of keys."

These very basic suggestions will not delve into the depths of the doctrines of the church or explore the nuances that have accompanied the Christian tradition. There are resources aplenty for anyone who wishes to explore those avenues and their many-faceted interpretations of the faith experience. This set of keys is more basic, but no less important. They provide helpful access to the rooms of theology and a perspective for dealing with what is found there, so that the encounters can be a healthy and wholesome part of the faith journey.

There are two particular features of the theological enterprise that have prompted me to offer these suggestions. One is an insight deep in our theological history, attributed to eleventh-century theologian Anselm of Canterbury. He defined theology as *fides quaerens intellectum* ("faith seeking understanding"), which suggests and presupposes a faith experience, but also assumes that its understanding is an ongoing quest rather than a fixed formula. This implies that theology is always a work in progress that, like any arena of understanding, will evolve in response to one's openness to new discoveries and insights.

Anselm's understanding of theology also implies that it is not the exclusive province of the clerics and the scholars, although they provide a valuable and necessary service in the maintenance of the tradition that carries the generations of the family of faith through history. Their work is not a substitute for the reflection and nurturing of a personal understanding of the faith experience and its application to life. "Every pilgrim a theologian" is an apt slogan for this point, and it is an assumption that underlies this offering of some basic and essential keys for engaging in the process.

The second "prompt" for what follows has resulted from some retirement reflection on fifty years of teaching in the field of religious studies, mostly at the undergraduate level, and mostly with students who were taking courses to satisfy general education requirements. These students would represent a reasonable cross section of the general population in terms of their religious experience and affiliations. Some were vocationally focused on further, more specialized study; and their commitments provided a basis for longer and continued association. But most were my traveling companions for one term, and our agenda was an introduction to religion in general, to the Bible, to Christian thought, or to Christian ethics. Levels of interest varied, of course, from resentment at having to take a course that had so little to do with their future plans, to a claimed interest in an opportunity to study something that had surrounded their lives but had not been a subject of careful scrutiny. I always hoped that we might spark some interest that would continue beyond the scope and schedule of the course, giving attention to the religious dimension of life and its place in both personal and public arenas.

The range of backgrounds of students was always interesting. Some students embraced and held dear the religious teachings experienced in childhood and were quite familiar with the stories and general beliefs of their particular traditions. Other students had grown weary with certain features of their backgrounds and had generally abandoned any thought about them. Some had never encountered in a serious way persons of a faith tradition different from their own, while yet others had observed the ways in which religious concepts could be "weaponized" and exploited in various ways to support other agendas.

That mix of experience usually led to meaningful discoveries about the diversity of religious experience and its application to life, and to an appreciation for the companionship of one another on the semester-long leg of the academic journey. I frequently heard these parting words: "I didn't really want to take this course, but I'm glad I did." There were, of course, memorable exceptions.

I describe this context at some length to characterize the present project as a response to my own discovery over the years that there are some very basic concepts, perspectives, and discernments that underlie an effort to understand faith in a healthy, maturing way. If I were doing my teaching efforts over again, these are some things on which I would spend more time at the beginning of every course, suggesting that these "keys" would be helpful in opening ways of thinking about topics that have both the blessing and the challenge of being familiar and often dearly held.

What this exercise will be, then, is an identification of some simple concepts, and some distinctions that are built into them, that sometimes don't appear in ordinary conversation. They are not complex or sophisticated., but they do require some precision of thought in their distinctions that matter a great deal in the ongoing process of "faith seeking understanding."

I hope you will not be put off by the seeming simplicity of the reflections that follow. I can anticipate the frequent response, "Of course we know that." I ask your patience to work through the implications of each of the "keys" to see their relevance for the task of understanding—and for helping others to understand—the faith we share. Many of the "theological conflicts" that challenged students in the formal study of religion found resolution in the embrace, absorption, and application of these basic conceptual tools. I believe much of the tension in the larger public discourse about religion would be lessened if adherents were to understand them.

When I was a seminary student more than a half-century ago, we were asked to read a little book by the German theologian Helmut Thielicke titled *A Little Exercise for Young Theologians*. It was described by preface writer Martin Marty, himself an esteemed historical theologian, as a kind of "greeting card" for aspiring ministers, offering simple yet profound principles and perspectives, along with warnings of attitudinal pitfalls, for those who would assume roles of leadership in the faith community. I found it helpful then, and it has been a helpful re-read over the years as the context of the Christian faith and the function of Christian theology have experienced dramatic changes.

While in no sense presuming to offer the kind of insights contained in that classical invitation to the formal theological profession, I have thought of the suggestions that follow as a kind of "Little Exercise for Everyday Theologians." Perhaps in spirit, if not in substance, you will find the invitation to be a "greeting card" for the theological endeavor that belongs to us all.

Part 1

Keys for Personal Discernment

Key #1—
Faith and Theology

To start with a very basic point, let's think about the reality that faith is and the process that theology is. "Faith" has many descriptions and definitions, and there is a need to be careful in what we mean by the term and how we use it in conversation and teaching. A quick look at a thesaurus will reveal there are many words in our language that can serve as synonyms for "faith": acceptance, belief, confidence, conviction, certitude, loyalty, commitment, allegiance, assurance, credence, fidelity, reliance, trust.

All of these are legitimate uses of the word, and their nuances indicate the shades of meaning to which they point. For our purposes, we will want to sharpen the focus of the term to point clearly to the "faith" that is the basis for our religious devotion and commitment. Generally speaking, the faith that is the heart of our Christian tradition is a relational term, pointing to the comprehensive relationship of persons to God (comprehensive in the sense that it is not just intellectual, emotional, or behavioral, but incorporating all aspects of what it means to be human—our "whole selves").

In the foundational covenant faith of Israel, the relational dimension is dominant; and the New Testament's portraits of Jesus and the emerging theology of the early church emphasize the centrality of faith as relationship. The central "greatest" commandments—"Love the Lord your God with all your heart, mind, soul and strength, and your neighbor as yourself"—lift the relational nature of faith to top priority as a way of understanding it. Beliefs are important, of course, as are behaviors and attitudes; but their importance is derived from their being expressions of this more basic relational reality.

Therefore, faith, in the sense that we use it theologically, is essentially a covenantal relationship, analogous to marriage, to deep friendship, and to various other partnerships whose meaning lies deep in the experience of the parties and is not limited to more surface contractual terms.

Now, if this is what faith is, then "faith seeking understanding" is the process of discerning the meaning and implications of the relationship and of the other party. This is the process of theology.

Familiarly, "theo-logy" is the combination of the two Greek words *Theos* (God) and *logos* (the "organizing principle of the universe"). When "logy" is added to a word, it suggests "making sense of" or "exploring the meaning of" the word that goes before. Psychology, sociology, biology, geology, and so on are among the many fields of study that reflect this focus.

Theology, then, is exploring the meaning of God and all that is involved in a relationship with God. Formally, the result of this effort to understand and give expression to God and a faith relationship is an accumulating body of interpretations and formulations that begin as personal testimonies of the faith experience, then expand to become confessions of faith shared by communities of similar experience, then tend to formalize into "doctrines" that give more standardized expression to the meaning of the faith. These doctrines can continue to move in an authoritative direction and become creeds and "dogma"—official (and enforceable) teaching that constitutes "orthodoxy" (right belief).

experience ⇨ testimony ⇨ shared confession ⇨ doctrines ⇨ creeds ⇨ dogma ⇨ orthodoxy

On a personal level, where our present theological concern is focused, these formalized interpretations have an influential role in an individual pilgrim's early framework for understanding the meaning of a personal faith. The "theological packaging" in which early guidance for a faith participant, whether in childhood or later, becomes the way in which the experience of faith is understood, reflected upon, and applied to life. When asked about one's faith, the answer will most likely come in terms of these concepts and language.

As helpful as these frameworks are for helping faith participants have the conceptual currency for speaking of their faith, there is a built-in danger in that helpfulness. What sets out to point to, describe, and invite thought about an experience of a relationship with God can easily become a definition of that experience and slip into being a substitute for the experience itself. A transforming faith experience, where one's orientation to life and one's way of seeing the world and all that is in it is changed at its core, can become focused on a particular way of speaking and thinking about it, to the point that certain expressions become the primary thing in bearing witness to the experience.

I think you can see the problem of focusing on saying the right things about Jesus, rather than seeking to refine one's understanding of God that comes from following Jesus. Formulas can be helpful expressions of what a faith relationship means, but they are not a good substitute for that relationship. In other words, doctrines can provide good and helpful light for the path, but they do not take the place of walking it.

A simplified and alliterative way of thinking about this relationship of faith and the "work" of theologians—formal ones and everyday ones—might be to observe that there are three "P's" of theology: perspective, process, and product. The faith experience itself provides the necessary prerequisite perspective. What we have been describing as the ongoing task of refining one's understanding of that experience is the process. The resulting interpretations and their formulation in doctrines are the product. As long as all three P's maintain a dynamic relationship with each other, good theology is being done. When a focus gets placed on any one at the expense of the other, the faith-theology partnership falters.

So here is the essence of this first key: theology is derived from faith and is the result of its expression and understanding at any point along the faith journey. It is a "describer" of faith, but not a "definer" of it. It is a pointer to faith's features and dynamics, but not a container of them. When the "cart gets before the horse," the process of faith seeking understanding gets its priorities out of order. And, we need to admit that this can happen at all levels of theological engagement, even the formal and sophisticated ones.

Application:
What stays locked in our theological thinking if this key of faith and theology is not used?

If the distinction between faith as relationship and theology as reflection and interpretation of that relationship is not made carefully, a number of obstacles can develop along the path of faith's journey. To put the point simply, relationships—especially significant and longstanding ones—have a profound, perhaps even mysterious reality to them that cannot be captured in language or concepts. Words and ideas can at best only point beyond themselves to the depth of the relationship in question: they can never completely define or contain all the dimensions that a relationship can be.

To use our earlier reference to the "three P's" of theology—perspective, process, and product—faith can sometimes be identified with one of the three, or all three together. Faith that is limited to the prerequisite perspective of the initial faith commitment can lead one to think that an embrace of the good news of God's work of grace in Jesus Christ is all there is to the faith experience. One is "saved" by that embrace, secure in one's relationship with God, and there is nothing more to it. The superficial analogy would be to say that birth is all there is to life.

To continue pointing to what stays locked if this key is not used, faith can become identified exclusively with the "process" of theological work. The what and how of theological thinking can become separated from the why—both the why of foundation and the why of purpose. Faith then becomes a matter of one's sophistication and fluency in the language and concepts of the discipline of theology, and a preoccupation with that fluency can become a detriment to the relationship it seeks to express.

If faith becomes too closely identified with the "product" of theological reflection, the normalized interpretations and doctrinal frameworks of faith's "official" understandings take on an authority that can usurp faith's authentic quest for understanding the depths of the relationship in the changing world of time and experience. Accepting authoritative definitions of a relationship is not the same as authentic participation in the relationship itself.

A related distinction within the practice of theology grows out of attention to the accumulated products of theological reflection. It is good and helpful to know how faith has been thought about by both formal and informal theologians through the generations. Insights and understandings from theology's "products" (i.e., doctrines) are valuable parts of the "trail guide" of faith's quest for understanding. The important distinction here is the difference between "knowing theology" and "thinking theologically."

The first is the knowledge of understandings that have resulted from theology's quest (important knowledge certainly), and the latter is a way of thinking that is characterized by discernments and disciplines that enable one to see beyond the foundations of accumulated knowledge and to be open to refinements of meaning that emerge from the quest. Some of these disciplines will be spelled out in the keys that follow.

Our first key hopefully unlocks the distinction between the faith experience and the theological process—and between knowing theology and thinking theologically— helping us to see the dynamic relationship between the two.

Key #2—
Faith and Beliefs

Closely related to this first key on the nature of faith and theology is a second one that helps us refine the relationship of two familiar concepts that are regular components of the theological task: faith and beliefs.

We have looked already at the centrality of faith as a relationship, and we suggested the analogy of marriage, friendship and other partnerships that have deep commitments. Such relationships are characterized by commitment, trust, respect, and concern for the well-being of the other party to the relationship.

Meaningful relationships have a life of their own. They are birthed in an experience of mutual discovery, have their "infancy" and childhood in early experiences, and grow toward maturity over time and with the challenges and rewards of experience. Few if any relationships stay the same throughout their lifetime, nor do the parties themselves. This is the relational metaphor through which we generally understand the meaning of religious faith.

"Faith" and "belief" are often used interchangeably in thinking and speaking about religious experience, and that is natural and easy to understand, given the way these terms have become familiar. But I want to suggest here as the second "key" a distinction that can help with some of the tensions that occur as we do our theological work.

Let's start with faith as the relationship we have described. Beliefs, then, are the understandings and concepts that accompany that relationship as it moves and grows over time. At the beginning of a marriage, for example, the parties to the marriage have certain concepts and understandings of what marriage is and what it means. Also, they have certain understandings of each other that have accompanied their relationship to that point. We can understand that these beliefs are authentic perceptions of where they are in their experience of the relationship. In this sense they are "true" beliefs.

It is easy to understand that as the relationship matures—and hopefully deepens and becomes more profound—some (perhaps many) of the beliefs that accompanied the partners at the beginning give way to more refined ones that benefit from the insights gained about the nature of marriage and about the partner with whom it is shared. We would think it odd if a person who has been married for a long time were to say, "My understanding of marriage and of my partner is exactly the same as it was the day we got married."

You see where this is going as a way of thinking about the journey of faith. The faith experience has its early stages and matures with time and experience to new levels of understanding. From the beginning, there are concepts and ideas that accompany the experience and provide the framework for understanding what it means. With the maturing of perspective and the expanding of knowledge, these accompanying ideas take on newer and more accurate forms to accommodate the maturing relationship.

The importance of the distinction between the relationship of faith and the beliefs that accompany it is seen when earlier beliefs are allowed to take on an authority that suggests they must be held against any insight that might suggest their refinement. To put it simply, *faith in God* (a trusting covenant relationship) can drift in the direction of allowing certain *beliefs about God* (concepts and ideas that accompany the relationship) to become authoritative in defining what the relationship must be.

To broaden the scope of this distinction a bit, it becomes important in other areas of theological reflection. A decision to follow Jesus is a faith commitment, while beliefs about Jesus will evolve over the course of the journey. Consider another example: embracing the authority of the Bible as a foundational testimony of covenant faith will experience many refinements of understanding with careful study of its history and development.

A familiar experience to illustrate this could be summarized in the tension that occurs when one studies a particular topic and finds that the results of that study call into question some beliefs about the subject earlier held. Letting go of a previously held belief in response to a new discovery can feel like a "loss of faith" (perhaps the kind about which one has been warned by well-meaning earlier mentors); and the tendency to want to defend the belief against the "new" insight is natural and understandable.

As we will see in our consideration of a later key, this fusion of faith and beliefs can be seen on large scale in the sixteenth century Church's defense of the geocentric "biblical" worldview of Aristotle and Ptolemy against the observations in support of a heliocentric solar system by Copernicus and Galileo. This belief about the structure of the universe accompanied the religious affirmation of God's creation of the world; and, when its accuracy was challenged by new discoveries, accepting its accuracy became a requirement for claiming a "creation faith."

On a smaller scale, the personal challenges to beliefs woven into one's background in the faith community, when broader vantage points and deeper investigation reveal their limitations, may be less historically dramatic; but they are no less real and challenging.

The key that can help unlock this challenge of a growing faith and the changing beliefs that accompany it is simply a clear awareness of how a deepening and maturing faith will naturally experience a refinement of beliefs. To make the point negatively, one of the main obstacles to a growing faith is a rigidity of belief.

Application:
What stays locked in our theological thinking if this key of faith and beliefs is not used?

If theology is faith seeking understanding, and if this key is not used, the "seeking" part can be neglected; and the task of theology becomes "faith defending a particular understanding." The "open-endedness" of the life of faith can be replaced by a closed system of beliefs that at one point of the process were perhaps quite authentic and sincere expressions of the faith experience. A belief system that remains "locked" from a

relationship's maturing refinements can have a crippling effect on the relationship's fulfillment of its creative possibilities.

On the larger stage of religious communities and the dynamics that exist with them,
the lack of ability or willingness to use this key is a major contributing factor to the
appeal and prevalence of various forms of fundamentalism. Closed beliefs that satisfy
and provide security for the faith relationship require less effort to embrace than does the
sometimes-uncertain path of pursuing the questions that naturally occur in the living of
that relationship in a context of an ever-changing environment. Allowing certain beliefs
to be the focus of one's ultimate loyalty, rather than being the tentative supports to one's
deeper loyalty, could be described as a kind of "conceptual idolatry"—a "golden calf" of
ideas and concepts in the wilderness of the covenant journey.

Key #3—
Faith and the Partiality of Understanding

Beneath the surface of the first key of the relation of faith and theology and the second key and its distinction between faith and beliefs is a principle that we will call our third key. If we were to give it a fancy philosophical name, we would say it is in the arena of "epistemology"—our understanding of, or making sense of, knowledge (*episteme*).

Remembering our starting point in the faith experience, this key has to do with what we claim to know on the basis of it and how we can best understand the nature of that knowledge, so that we can claim enough but not too much for what we have.

To put it simply, consider the difference between a reality of some kind and our understanding of that reality. For example, on the surface there is not much about an ordinary pencil that we cannot understand: it is a cylindrical piece of wood with a thin shaft of graphite in the middle that can be sharpened to expose a point that will transfer to a paper or other surface and a cap on the other end holding a rubber eraser to use to correct mistakes. The percentage of the reality of the pencil that we can understand is pretty high (maybe 95 percent?). Components such as the kind of tree the wood came from and the molecular composition of the graphite might make up the "unknown" parts.

Even with this simple example, we would not likely claim to know everything there is to know about a pencil. Our concept of the pencil will always be a partial or less complete portrayal of the reality of the pencil itself.

Now, let's upgrade the complexity of our "reality" to the squirrel who is sitting on a limb of the tree outside the window. My "concept" of squirrel is adequate enough for me to recognize it and to have some sense of its place in the animal world, but the percentage of my "concept of squirrel" to the "reality of squirrel" is quite a bit lower. If I were a zoologist or a veterinarian, my concept would be closer to the reality, but even specialists would probably admit to a partiality of understanding.

To take this idea a step further, think of a nine-year-old boy playing in the yard next door. My concept of nine-year-olds in general is supplemented by my personal knowledge of him and our relationship as neighbors since he was about four. To say that my concept of him is only a partial picture of who he is would be obvious. There is much more to the reality (and mystery) of this fine young man than I can know.

If we were to lift our consideration beyond physical realities to more abstract ones such as friendship, love, justice and faith, our concepts of these realities would be limited to our experience with them and also clearly partial.

The point is obvious by now: The more complex the reality, the more partial is our understanding of it.

The relevance of this "epistemological key" to the theological task is easy to see, and apparently easy to forget to use, in many religious claims that reflect a sense of certainty that one has understood the realities of God and the spiritual life.

Religious experience tends to be consuming and comprehensive from a personal standpoint. It involves our whole being; no part of our existence is exempt from its effects. It is not just an intellectual, or physical, or emotional, or even narrowly "spiritual" experience; it is a full engagement of all aspects of who we are.

Since there is little if anything in our experience that is outside its framework, it is understandable that we might assume that others will experience it in the same way. Especially if we are part of a community that shares the same pattern of experience and its understanding, we develop a standardized way of expressing and understanding our faith.

The first expressions of challenge to that understanding usually occur in encounters with persons from other communities of faith or in the study of the broader world of religious experience. We find in that challenge that different people can look at something with the same label ("religious experience") and see different things and understand it in different ways.

This happens so frequently in our diverse and religiously pluralistic world that it seems artificial to separate out a "before and after" profile of the process. But it seems helpful here to clarify the point that what we see and understand about anything, especially something as consuming as religious faith, has the distinctive feature of our vantage point, and there is no vantage point from which one can see all there is to see about the thing seen.

I live near the remarkable geologic phenomenon known as Stone Mountain. Everyone around here knows what it is and can readily identify it anytime a picture of it is shown. The interesting thing about the mountain is that if it is viewed from any of the four compass point directions, it looks quite different. From the north, it seems to be a gray wall, rising almost vertically 800 feet or so above the surrounding terrain. From the west, it looks like a wooded mountain with a bald top. From the south, it appears to be a large tan hill rising gradually from its base to its summit. And from the east, it looks like a large grey football sitting on the horizon.

If a person from each of these vantage points were asked to describe the mountain, the resulting pictures would be different. To the question, "Which one is right?" our answer would naturally be: "All are, but each one is only part of the picture of the full reality of the mountain."

To theological questions—for example: "What is the meaning of faith?" "What is God like?" "Who is Jesus Christ?" "What is the church?" "What does it mean to be human?" "What is the destiny of history?"—we have a similar pattern of diverse vantage points and consequent partial understandings of realities that pull us beyond the limitations of our original impressions.

This recognition of the partiality of our concepts of realities and of our understanding of them is the key that unlocks the door to the essential virtue of theological humility—that feature of our "faith's seeking understanding" that recognizes the influence and limitation of the vantage point on what one sees and the importance of considering the possibility and the benefit of finding community with those of other vantage points. We will return to unlocking that room with another key later.

Application:
What stays locked in our theological thinking if this key of faith and the partiality of understanding is not used?

The area of our theological thinking where this key is most useful is in dealing with the question of the relation of one's faith to those of other faith traditions. The normal tendency, as we have suggested, is to assume that one's "home" understanding of something is the norm or standard by which other understandings are measured and evaluated. That assumption works just fine if one's context is limited to that one way of thinking and speaking. That kind of context no longer exists, especially in the arena of religious experience.

So significant and compelling is the nature of religious experience that it is not surprising that there can be a tendency to hold to its truth in such a way that other ways of being religious (or of understanding religion) are evaluated in terms of their similarity or rejected simply because they are different. This is the kind of "exclusivism" that claims truth for one's own faith and dismisses all others as false. There are varying forms of this exclusivism, of course—some harsher than others—but the common thread is the claim of superiority of one's own understanding and a resistance to the truth of that of others. "Can I be right if you're not wrong?" is the rhetorical question in this locked theological room.

We can see the challenge for theological conversation across lines of tradition if this key is not used, and we will address it further in a later section. Suffice it here to say that an earlier acquaintance and use of this key will make the theological path less stressful and more faithful as our awareness of the size and make-up of God's faith family broadens and deepens.

Key #4—
Faith and the Sources of Theological Guidance

Faith's ongoing quest for understanding is not without guidance. From the earliest steps of the journey and throughout its duration, there are resources that offer help on many levels in the quest. Since we are thinking primarily within the covenant faith of the Judeo-Christian tradition, we will work with the resources that are part of that context.

Most familiar and most frequently used are the foundational resources of scripture and the central teaching of the church, followed closely by the particular teachings of the part of the Christian family that is our personal connection (e.g., denomination). Then there is the wide range of guidance found in the prolific body of literature that speaks to the life of faith.

This fourth key for our theological work is intended to unlock a perspective for a healthy and effective use of these resources, to draw on the benefit they can and do provide as guides for the quest for understanding the relationship of faith.

Like keys for more sophisticated locks, this one is a little more complicated due to the nature of these source-guides and the significance assigned to them by parts of the Christian faith family. If we broaden our image a bit from the door to careful theological thinking that the first three keys open, we might think of the theological house having a number of rooms, each of which contains helpful guidance for continuing the quest. One might be the Bible, another the collective tradition and teaching of the church that developed over the centuries, another the commonly held understandings of our particular part of the faith family, and another our personal experience.

We need a key or keys here to help us know what these resources are and how most faithfully to use them. We will look at some specialized keys for these particular rooms of guidance in the theological house in later sections. Here we will look at the "general key" that will apply to each of the more specialized rooms: Be as careful and thorough as possible in understanding what the source of guidance is.

Understanding the nature of the source involves a careful discernment of just exactly what it is (often different from and behind a community's assessment of its significance), how it came to become a source of guidance, and where it fits in the overall framework of the faith community's life.

It goes without saying that honesty is a prerequisite to faithful theological work. Often, honesty requires that we refine understandings by exchanging concepts that no longer portray what they once did for concepts that point better to the reality in question. We can remember childhood images of various aspects of life and how they have changed with time and experience.

The Bible

To illustrate this principle with perhaps the most obvious example, an understanding of what the Bible is accompanies our faith journey from the earliest days of our pilgrimage. We are taught to see it as one of God's most important gifts, to respect it and to anticipate a lifetime of guidance from its teachings. We learn to speak of it as "God's Word" and to treat it with the reverence such a book is due. We learn its stories, memorize key verses, and are told of the life lessons derived from its pages. It frames the narrative by which we see ourselves as participants in the larger family of God's people.

If we are given the opportunity and encouragement to study the Bible carefully—the context of history out of which it comes, and the process by which it came to be what we now have before us—we broaden and deepen our concept of what it is from "God's word" to a much more complex and dynamic collection of writings that reflect the many generations-long experience of a community of people giving expression in multiple ways of a covenant relationship with a God whom they have experienced in their history.

Here we find an important subpoint to this key and its principle of honesty in dealing with a source of theological guidance. It is another "epistemological" distinction that often gets overlooked in experiences of Bible study. Put simply, it is the difference between a *description of* something and an *affirmation about* that something. Let's consider also a simple example:

Suppose we ask a friend to tell us about her son, whom we have not met, and she replies, "He is a 4-foot-tall, 65-pound, 7-year-old, with brown hair and brown eyes. He is in Miss Smith's second-grade class at Creekside Elementary School, and he is taking swimming lessons at our neighborhood pool." Notice that all of these statements are descriptions of the boy—facts whose accuracy can be verified by measuring, weighing, observing, checking school records, etc.

Now suppose this mom continues: "He is the light of our lives, a true gift of God to our family, and one whose life helps us understand the bigger picture of what family life is all about." Notice here that what she says are affirmations about her son. They are not verifiable by any kind of external means. These statements cannot be "proved" in any of the normal ways we verify information. They are statements about her son, to be sure, but they are also statements about the relationship that he shares with the rest of his family, which is a complex reality of physical, emotional, and even spiritual commitments that cannot be measured the way descriptive "facts" are.

Shifting back now to our thinking about the Bible as one of the sources of guidance for our theological work, if we are asked, "What is the Bible?" our answers will probably be a mixture of descriptions of and affirmations about this foundational support for our faith's understanding. Our earliest answers would probably reflect the guidance we first received about the Bible's importance: "God's holy inspired word," "all you need to know about life," "God's roadmap for the journey of life," "ultimate truth." Note that all of these labels and many others in a similar vein are affirmations about the Bible—statements that point to its significance and value, and that reflect the speaker's relationship with it.

If we were to say, "The Bible is the scripture of the Judeo-Christian tradition," or "a collection of writings grouped into two testaments," or "66 books that serve as an authority for churches in the Protestant tradition," or "the universal bestseller of all books published," we would be making statements that are descriptions of the Bible—statements that can be verified without reference to anyone's relationship with it.

Affirmations about the Bible's significance will be a "given" for those who engage in "faith seeking understanding" in the Christian family, even though those affirmations will most likely evolve with faith's maturing process. That is a natural part of the journey.

The importance of the descriptions of the Bible that accompany our use of its guidance is illustrated by how our descriptions can affect the way we understand and use it. The first descriptive answers to "what it is" are similar to the ones noted above (two testaments, 66 books, history of the Hebrew people and the early church, etc.). As our study of it naturally leads to other topics such as "how we got our Bible," we can begin to see how different descriptions can have an impact on our use of it.

Consider some different descriptive responses to the question of "how we got the Bible":

- "The Bible was written in heaven by God and dropped out of the sky to be read and followed by all people."
- "The Bible was written by individual authors directly inspired by God to write the words they wrote, and what we have is the result of that process."
- "The Bible is a collection of writings that bear witness to a diverse people's experience with God in their history over centuries of time and reflecting the cultural worldviews of their time."
- "The Bible is a developing expression of the religious experience of an ancient people, culminating in a vision for a future that will be characterized by what they came to understand God's intention in creation to be."

These statements are different descriptions of the process by which the Bible came to be, and they reflect understandings that are held by a range of people who embrace the Bible's authority and significance as a spiritual guide. It is easy to see how these understandings of "what the Bible is" will affect and be affected by a deeper study of its content and history of development.

A particular descriptive understanding of what the Bible is will also affect its function as a resource for theological thinking. Understanding it as "holy writ" (words directly from God) will lead to one kind of adherence (often a literal application of its words to specific questions and issues), while understanding it as an evolving testimony of a covenant community seeking to give expression of their experience with God will lead to a different kind of use (most often questions of how their experience and testimony shed light on the faith journey as it is experienced in other times).

So, this subkey to the biblical room of the theological house affirms the importance of a careful understanding of "what the Bible is" as a needed prerequisite to the long process of study of its many dimensions and a faithful exercise of its use.

There are many resources that are helpful for additional reflection and study on this particular point (for "cutting this subkey"). One that I have found that is particularly helpful for both Bible reading veterans and newcomers to its literature is Marcus Borg's *Reading the Bible Again for the First Time*.[1]

Church Tradition

It is not surprising that the centuries of the church's life have accumulated understandings of faith that have been influential and helpful for subsequent generations. Shared understandings came to be formulated as "doctrines," usually assembled into "confessions of faith" (shared testimonies of the essentials of what it means to be Christian), often elevated to the status of "creeds" (official and authoritative understandings) that would be used to evaluate subsequent expressions of what the faith means.

The positive value of these "official" understandings is that each generation did not have to start from scratch in proclaiming and teaching the substance of its faith experience. There was a "trail guide" for the faith journey, with many questions already addressed and with answers already provided. The collective wisdom of the Christian community gradually evolved into a body of understanding that we call "orthodoxy" (meaning "right belief"), which became the standard by which expressions and application of the faith were evaluated.

The negative challenge of this orthodoxy and its various components is that they, like all formulations, reflect the values and perspective of the culture of their context; and, over time, the faith journey moves into different territory culturally and intellectually. To use an image from one of Jesus' sayings, the "old wineskins cannot contain the new wine" of faith's ongoing development. So, while the "accumulated wisdom" of the faith community's shared understanding provides a structure and framework for guidance in worship, education, and general reflection on the meaning of the faith, it also has a tentativeness and a flexibility about it that allow and encourage revision as new insights and applications emerge from faith's engagement with life in real time.

The longstanding relation of "conservative" and "liberal" perspectives embodies this dynamic of faith's foundation and its growing edge. Both are needed to sustain the roots and branches of the theological tree. A commitment to "conserve" what is of ongoing value and a commitment to be open to the need for ongoing refinement are essential partners in the work of theology.

As we noted the importance of a careful understanding of "what the Bible is" as a basis for a faithful use of it as a source of guidance for theological thinking, it is equally important to understand the established tradition of the church for "what it is." The tradition's own claims of authority need to be balanced with an awareness of its evolving nature as a valuable and helpful reading of the meaning of faith at a given time, in the concepts and language of that time, with an open-endedness for growth and change as new issues and insights emerge from engagement with the ongoing challenges of the journey.

A helpful resource for further reflection and information about the confessions and creeds of the church is a chapter titled "Who Says So? The Problem of Authority" in a book by Shirley Guthrie, *Christian Doctrine—Revised Edition*.[2]

Personal Experience and Community Engagement

Another less tangible, but still important, source of guidance for the theological task is one's own experience of faith's embrace. How that is seen and understood will vary from person to person. It involves a change of perspective and values, a reoriented way of relating to others, a sense of peace and security in relating to life in general, and a sense of relatedness to God that changes how one relates to everything else.

As we noted at the beginning of our discussion on faith and theology, this personal experience of faith is the starting point for theological reflection, for it is the meaning of that experience in its personal and expanded context upon which theological thinking is built.

Theological study can expand understanding of the personal experience of faith, but it does not take the place of it; and the experience itself is a reference point for any subsequent reflection on it. Here, again, it is important to understand this source of guidance for what it is, as we suggested for both the Bible and the accumulated teaching of the church.

It is helpful and important to acknowledge the subjective nature of personal experience—how values and prejudices will affect how we understand even transformative experiences. What we bring to the experience will find its way into how we interpret its significance and meaning.

For most people, personal faith is lived in the context of a faith community where persons of similar experience support and guide each other in the pilgrimage. The tone and spirit of such communities will have a significant effect on how faith is understood and how much encouragement (or lack of it) there will be for "faith to seek understanding" beyond its present framework. Much of the time, this faith community serves as the "midwife" at the birth of a faith experience and as the mothers and fathers of the faith experience as it moves from infancy, through its childhood and adolescence and into its adulthood. We will explore this process of faith development in an upcoming key,

Personal theological work, with its emphasis on its personal nature and integrity, most often will be done in the relationships of this community. The process of maturation from dependence and absorption of the community's shared understanding toward the relative independence and responsibility for the maintenance and responsible growth of that understanding is another facet of this key of clear understanding just what our sources of guidance are and how to be a faithful steward of them.

But there is a challenge here: The question of what happens if and when one's personal theological thinking moves outside the parameters of one's "home" spiritual community—the faith family that midwifed one's birth and nurtured one's growing faith toward maturity—will be discussed in a later section on the key of faith and personal growth. This is not an uncommon occurrence, and one that is laden with both stress and creative possibility.

Application:
What remains locked if this key of faith and sources of theological guidance is not used?

An honest and informed perception of what a source of guidance for faith's understanding is helps the theologian to use it appropriately. An implicit granting of supreme authority to the Bible as a repository of divine truth, or to church tradition as an infallible guide for right belief, or to personal experience and community patterns as the only valid expressions of faith can lead to a subtle but real form of idolatry that focuses commitment and loyalty to the guide rather than to the relational journey to which it points. Once locked into that kind of commitment, theological thinking tends to become a defense of certain perceptions of the guide rather than a use of the guide to assist with the ongoing quest for understanding faith.

Key #5—

Faith and the Religious Marketplace

Closely related to our key for unlocking honesty and clarity for our primary sources of guidance, there is some secondary guidance that will vie for our attention and commitment.

Faith seeking understanding can easily be overwhelmed by the abundance of books and articles that address the issues and challenges that appear at the intersection of faith and life. From the ancient classics to the latest bestsellers and everything in between, there are more resources for guidance available than anyone could ever absorb. And, it would be impossible to offer a basic key that would suggest "read this" or "buy that." What our Key #5 might do is suggest a principle that can perhaps best be illustrated with an analogy from the world of nutrition.

There are lots of different kinds of foods available for us to eat. Some are less expensive, some are more. Some taste better and are more enjoyable to eat than others. Foods have different levels of nutritional value. Sometimes research finds that certain foods can be harmful to health, while certain foods are helpful to people who have various medical conditions. Put simply, some food nourishes our well-being while some food is either somewhat irrelevant to it or even harmful to it. There is food that is part of a healthy diet, and there is "junk food"—tasty and enjoyable, but negligible or even harmful in excess to our health.

In the arena of theological guidance, it should not surprise us that there is good nourishment for our faith's seeking understanding and other, less nourishing, perhaps even misleading "theological food" that can lead to a stymying of the quest or a following of a less healthy path of thought.

A concern for a healthy "faith diet" would lead us to find a way of evaluating the offerings of the religious marketplace in terms of their nutritional value for our thinking about faith. This is tricky, because such an evaluation risks imposing preconceived concepts of what is healthy and wholesome upon theological guidance, accepting or rejecting it on the basis of one's preconceived ideas, rather than upon the possibility of help in the quest for understanding. In our shopping for "theological nourishment," is there a way to make choices that are fair to what is offered and at the same time careful as to their value as theological guidance?

With the assumption that there is a difference between healthy faith and theological reflection on it, and unhealthy faith and its accompanying theology, the question becomes: How can we discern that difference? Some would suggest certain "belief tests" for evaluating such guidance: "Does this resource believe this about God, or about Jesus, or about the nature of humankind?" "Does it believe this about the Bible?" "Does it align with the time-honored doctrinal framework of Christian orthodoxy?" Such belief tests would lay a conceptual template over a resource for theological guidance and evaluate its worth in terms of its correspondence with what the template prescribes.

Working over the years with students on the idea of healthy and unhealthy religion—of which there were always available examples in the news of the day—we found it helpful to clarify our own thinking by pondering how we would complete the sentence, "A healthy religious perspective is one that…" We could easily find examples of what we would consider unhealthy religious faith, such as a faith community that advocated abuse of children, or embraced rigid beliefs and prejudices that excluded persons who had experienced various kinds of failures or were "different" in other ways. Translating those negative observations into positive principles would result in well-conceived characteristics of what a healthy religious understanding would be: "A healthy religion respects and nourishes the integrity and well-being of children." Or, "A healthy religion offers hospitality and restoration to persons who have need of acceptance and forgiveness for past mistakes."

Shaping a concept of a "healthy" faith and using it as a guide for evaluating religious guidance is a life-long process, refined by experience and critical reflection on how one's faith weaves its way through all of life's experiences.

To help this process along, we found a helpful resource by psychologist/theologian Howard Clinebell in a section of his book *The Mental Health Ministry of the Local Church* (Nashville: Abingdon Press, 1965, pp. 30-54). He offers there some questions that can serve as "tests" for what he calls a "mentally healthy" religious faith. We could use them as questions to guide us in our evaluation of the "healthiness" or "theological nutritional value" of available guidance in the marketplace. Clinebell asks if a particular form of religious thought and practice…[3]

- builds bridges or barriers between people
- strengthens or weakens a basic sense of trust and relatedness to the universe
- stimulates or hampers the growth of inner freedom and personal responsibility
- encourages healthy or unhealthy dependency relationships
- encourages growth of mature or immature consciences
- provides effective or faulty means of helping persons move from a sense of guilt to forgiveness
- provides well-defined, significant guidelines or emphasizes ethical trivia
- is primarily concerned for surface behavior or for the underlying health of the personality
- increases or lessens the enjoyment of life
- encourages a person to appreciate or deprecate the feeling dimension of life
- handles vital energies of sex and aggressiveness in constructive or repressive ways?
- encourages the acceptance or denial of reality
- fosters magical or mature religious beliefs

- encourages intellectual honesty with respect to doubts
- oversimplifies the human situation or faces its tangled complexity
- emphasizes love (and growth) or fear
- gives its adherents a "frame of orientation and object of devotion" (Erich Fromm) that is adequate in handling existential anxiety constructively
- encourages the individual to relate to his unconscious through living symbols (finding ways to connect with life's deeper meanings)
- accommodates itself to the neurotic patterns of the society or endeavors to change them
- strengthens or weakens self-esteem

According to Clinebell, "a particular form of religious belief and practice enhances mental health (is healthy) when it builds bridges between people, strengthens the sense of trust, stimulates inner freedom, encourages the acceptance of reality, builds respect for both the emotional and intellectual levels of life, increases the enjoyment of life, handles sex and aggressiveness constructively, is concerned for the health of personality (rather than surface symptoms), provides effective means of handling guilt, emphasizes growth and love, provides an adequate frame of reference and object of devotion, relates to persons with their unconscious minds, endeavors to change neurotic patterns of society, and enhances self-esteem."[4]

Questions such as the ones Clinebell poses can help us select and evaluate among the wide range of resources available in the religious marketplace to help us as guides in our ongoing theological quest for faith's understanding.

Additional personal help in the process of selecting resources for this cultivation of discernment would be the insights of trusted and experienced companions in the faith journey. There are no easy short-cuts for developing the experience of good judgment in the selection of resources to read and study. Guidance shared by fellow theologians from their experience can sharpen the stewardship of time and effort in one's own quest for understanding.

Application:
What stays locked in our theological thinking if this key of faith and the religious marketplace is not used?

Discernment is the key. In the religious marketplace, just as in other arenas where products are sold, careful marketing is used to draw consumers to buy what is available. The ebb and flow of fad and fashion, the creativity of appeals to needs and desires, and the reputation of the marketer all combine to appeal to the buyer and to sell the product. The less one knows about the product—its nature and its purpose—the more vulnerable one is to being manipulated into buying something that may not live up to its claims.

The more informed a consumer is, the more likely he or she is to discern the value of the product for use.

Knowledge and careful thinking work together to produce discernment, and that discernment is what is unlocked and available for helpful use in the marketplace of theological guidance. Without it, in a world where misinformation and outright falsehoods flood public communication, the everyday theologian is vulnerable to misinformation and misleading advice. Everyone needs the help of others in this arena of theological work.

Key #6—
Faith and the Levels of Truth

Our previous key of discernment assumes that faith seeking understanding will work toward being able to assess the truthfulness of religious claims and to select the guidance that will provide reliable assistance for following the pathways of faith. Being able to recognize what is "true" and committing oneself to the truth of the faith community's guiding testimony are essential features of theological work.

This opens another area of epistemological concern that benefits from some careful consideration of what "truth" is and how we think about what is true.

At the risk of offending with simplicity, let's start with some basic ways of thinking about truth. Suppose I say, "It is raining outside." Is my statement true, and how would you determine whether it is or not? It is either true or false, and it can be verified simply by looking outside to see. Or, if we ask, "Is Charles at school today?' and his mother says "Yes," the truth of her answer can be checked with some certainty—he either is or he isn't.

Truth in these examples is essentially factual accuracy, based on commonly accepted means of verification. If I claim that it is raining when it is not, or if Charles is skipping school without his mother's knowledge, the statements are not true—they do not accurately represent the facts.

Factual accuracy is the most basic level of truth, and we rely on it naturally and easily in everyday life for information that is of value to us. We value what is true and we dismiss and evaluate negatively what is false. If a product claims to clean stains from clothing, and it does not, we dismiss the claim as untrue and do not buy the product.

Beyond such simple examples, truth as factual accuracy can have broader implications. In the arena of historical information, for example, truth is expanded to apply to whether reports of events and processes of history are accurately portrayed, on the basis of the evidence that is available. Times and places of important events, and biographical details of important characters can be assessed as to whether they are accurate or not, when data is available; and there is an honest admission of uncertainty when verifying data are not there. Sometimes what was understood as factually accurate turns out not to be, when additional evidence is discovered that changes the understanding of the relevant facts. A "truthful" response acknowledges the correction and embraces the new understanding. Again, the truth of a historical report lies in whether or not its information is accurate.

An additional level of "historical truth" involves whether a particular portrayal is complete and accurate. A portrayal can contain accurate information, but for a variety of reasons may not contain additional information that changes the overall picture of what is portrayed. Accounts of conflicts, for example, might offer a version that represents a view of only one side—accurate enough factually, but limited and not balanced by a version as seen by the other side. Historical scholarship is constantly seeking to refine its portrayals by the inclusion of data yet undiscovered or deliberately underemphasized. A "true" portrayal will be both accurate and open to refinement as evidence leads.

We encounter other "levels" of truth when we move into dimensions of life that are not limited to provable facts, where meaning enters as a feature of truth in addition to accuracy. Thinking and speaking of things such as responsibility, loyalty, morality, and religious faith go deeper than the surface of factual accuracy; and this is where "truth" becomes an issue in need of careful discernment in theological work.

Let's use a simple illustration: Aesop's famous fable of the tortoise and the hare. Once upon a time, a rabbit and a turtle are involved in a discussion of who is the better runner. To settle the question, they decide to have a race. At the starting signal, the rabbit takes off with great speed, leaving the turtle woefully behind. After a bit, the rabbit decides he doesn't need to try so hard and stops to take a nap beside the road. Meanwhile the turtle continues his slow and steady pace, quietly passing the sleeping rabbit on toward the finish line. The rabbit wakes just in time to see the tortoise reach and cross the finish line just before he himself can get there, winning the race and settling the question of who is the better runner.

Is this story true? If we think of "true" in the sense of factual accuracy, most probably not—there is no reason to believe that such an event could occur as portrayed. But, is it true on another level? If the story is not really about two animals having a race, but instead about the difference between slow, steady, and determined effort and rapid careless effort that loses sight of its purpose, then we might say there is a significant truth there.

The point of this illustration and this key for theological thinking is that there are levels of truth we recognize in everyday life that enable us to claim "truthfulness" for features of life that cannot be measured by the criteria of factual accuracy. These deeper levels of truth are most often communicated by stories, fables, parables, legends, and sagas that become vehicles for truths that are not limited to the particular images that carry the story.

Perhaps the most familiar expressions of this kind of truth are the children's stories that plant seeds of responsibility, curiosity, and respect in memorable ways that "grow up" into the virtues that we hope they will embrace as they develop. We don't expect children to maintain a literal understanding of a story that they will someday grow beyond, but we hope the truth at the deeper level of the story will have formative and sustaining influence in their thinking and living.

It may be obvious why I am suggesting this rather simple point as a "key" for theological thinking. On the surface it might seem that everyone understands that there are many levels of truth that find their way into our experience by stories, art, poetry, drama, and other means of introducing and nurturing ideas and values that create the depth of human experience. But wait, let's think about …

Application:
What stays locked in theological thinking if this key of faith and the levels of truth is not used?

Oddly, it seems that sometimes religious devotion and religious thinking find themselves confined to a one-dimensional concept of truth, where if something is not true on the factual accuracy level, it cannot be true at all. Quite often, this challenge is found in the study of the biblical testimony, where the truth it points to is sometimes expressed in language and images that are culturally conditioned by their time and place, and may not reflect what would later be understood to be factual or historical accuracy.

As understandings of the world evolve over time in the development of history, reflecting the discoveries that are the natural processes of human curiosity and study, earlier understandings are recognized as limited and in need of refinement. Faith can and should celebrate those refinements as the fruit of a God-given ability to study, learn, and be stewards of the calling to have dominion over the created order (Gen. 1:26-27).

Religious "faith truth" lies in the authenticity of the relationship that embraces the covenant promise, "I will be with you." The understandings of the world that accompany that relationship grow and change with time. If theology (faith seeking understanding) finds itself moving from an effort to understand the deepening truth of the relationship to defending the truth (accuracy) of the understandings that accompany it, time and energy will be focused on something other than faith itself.

We will see a more extensive discussion of a version of this key in the next section, which will consider a concern that is a frequent arena of theological challenge.

Key #7—

Faith and Science

In looking at conceptual keys for this part of our theological thinking, we will wade into the sometimes-thorny issue of the relation of religion and science. This has been a topic of some controversy since the sixteenth century, when a mathematician and astronomer named Nicholaus Copernicus challenged the traditional understanding of the structure of the universe. With several pivotal battles over the years since, it has continued to be an arena of stress and misunderstanding, even to the present.

Everyday theologians encounter this issue when questions arise over the truth of the biblical stories of creation, or of certain events in the testimony that portray natural phenomena that strain the modern mind to accept as presented. The issue often leads to a confrontation that requires one to "have enough faith" to accept the truth of something that is contrary to facts as known. The cartoonish version of the situation is captured in the youngster's definition of faith: "Faith is believing something that you know ain't so."

The irony of the conflict is that it is really quite unnecessary, and it is usually the result of some misunderstandings (or lack of understanding) of some very basic principles of how we think and how we respond to our world. These basic principles comprise a subset of keys for theological thinking that can be helpful as we clarify for ourselves the particular nature of religious thinking and scientific thinking, with the hope that we might be helpful to others who will inevitably find themselves in places where the under-lying misunderstandings lead to the detriment of religion or science or both.

We will look in this section at two particular conceptual keys that have been helpful to students over the years in dealing with this challenge.

Imagine this scenario: A thousand years ago, a man and his child are standing at daybreak in a place where they have a wide view of the eastern sky. The sunrise is provid-ing a vivid display of brilliant colors, and they are quite taken by its wonder and beauty. The child asks, "Daddy, what makes the sky so pretty?" The father replies: "God and his angels stayed up all night painting the sky for us to enjoy when the sun comes up to shine on it. Isn't it beautiful?"

Now, imagine this scenario: Last summer, a mother and her child are at the beach on the Atlantic coast, and they get up to watch the sunrise. As they watch, the sky begins to light up with colors quite similar to those watched a millennium ago in our first scenario. They are both moved with wonder at nature's beauty. The child asks, "Mommy, what makes the sky so pretty?" The mother replies: "The sunlight shines through particles of dust and other material in the atmosphere, and that filtering effect produces some of the colors we see. And the water droplets in the clouds act like the prism in our suncatcher in the window at home and separate the light into its various colors. Isn't it beautiful?"

Let's think about these two scenarios for a moment: Let's assume that the two sunrises are reasonably similar in their displays of color and that the two parents and their children are similarly moved by the spectacular beauty before them. But we can't help noticing that their awe and wonder at the beauty of the sunrise is accompanied by two very different understandings of what has made this beauty happen. The medieval parent offers an explanation that would no doubt be quite common in his time, when natural phenomena were often understood to be the activity of divine beings; and this is his answer to the child's "how?" question. Although this parent's answer is inaccurate from our perspective, it is the best one he can provide. But notice that the inaccuracy of the answer from our modern scientific point of view does not seem to diminish the aesthetic experience of viewing the beauty of the sunrise and of being moved to reverence by it.

The twenty-first-century parent offers an explanation that reflects a modern understanding of light filtration and refraction, atmospheric conditions, and the rotation of the earth on its axis—all commonplace understandings in our time. Her answer to the child's "how?" question is the best one she can provide. It is much more accurate than the answer of the medieval parent, but we can also imagine that the awe and wonder of parent and child at the beauty of the sunrise is no more authentic.

These two hypothetical scenarios illustrate that when we respond to our world, especially our "natural" world, there are two distinct ways that we look at and think about what we are experiencing. A "religious" response and a "scientific" response are different, yet quite complementary responses to our world. If a conflict arises between them, it is because one or the other of them is trying to do the other one's work.

The Distinction Between "Descriptions of" and "Affirmations About"

In Key #4 we spoke about a friend's description of her son. Now, suppose that child is yours and I ask you to tell me about him. You respond: "He is a 9-year-old boy, with dark hair and brown eyes. He is 48 inches tall and weighs 65 pounds. He was born at Memorial Hospital on October 5, 2012. He is a student in Mrs. Smith's class at Creekside Elementary School, where he won the spelling bee for his grade level this year."

Notice that everything you have said about your son is a description of him—a report of facts that could be independently verified. Some of the facts I could check by observation (hair, eye color, gender, etc.). Others I could verify through public records (birthplace and date) or school records, and some with a ruler and a weight scale. In short, I could check the accuracy of everything you have said; and chances are that everything you have said is accurate.

Now, suppose you reply to my question in a different way: "My son is the light of my life, God's true gift to our family, and the center of my world. He helps me understand the true meaning of love and is the greatest treasure I could ever imagine."

Recall that what you have said this time is a series of affirmations about your son, none of which can be verified by external measurements or standards. They are expressions of the relationship you have with him, and they do not lend themselves to the kind of verification we noted above. Another way of distinguishing between the two kinds of statements would be to note that the descriptions are about your son, whereas the affirmations are about the relationship you have with him.

Now, let's apply this principle to our current topic of study: The scientific part of our thinking has to do with the descriptions that result from our observations and measurements of our world. We do not have to be "scientists" in the formal sense of the word to participate in scientific thinking. We measure and calculate all the time—such as when we observe and decide whether there is enough space between two cars for us to pull between them, or when we note the time and decide whether we can stop at the store before an appointment; or whether we have enough money this month to buy something we have wanted. Our "scientific" understandings are either accurate or inaccurate, and we spend our lives working to refine them, so that our judgments and decisions based on them will be better.

The non-scientific (here I'll say religious) part of our thinking has to do with the affirmations that give expression to our relationship with the things our scientific thinking describes. We generally do not think of these affirmations as being accurate or inaccurate, but as being authentic or inauthentic.

The point is, the scientific part of our thinking and the religious part of our thinking are distinct responses to our world: they both are important, and they don't compete with each other. It is hard to imagine a world without our ability to measure, calculate, and build things with the resources of chemistry, physics, and electronics; but it is also hard to imagine a world without the personal relationships that give life meaning. I would not want to choose between being scientific or being religious—I'm glad we don't have to.

How Science and Religion Work Together

A second conceptual discernment here builds on the first one. It can be stated simply: Every religious affirmation is accompanied by a particular scientific understanding. Let's unpack that briefly with the help of our two introductory scenarios.

When our medieval parent was moved to wonder and reverence at the beauty of the sunrise ("How beautiful God's world is!"), his affirmation was accompanied by an understanding of the world that ascribed to divine beings the direct cause of what he was seeing. We would not diminish the truth (authenticity) of his affirmation by noting the inaccuracy of the understanding of the natural world that accompanied it. We would simply recognize that he had not yet had the opportunity to learn some things that we have been privileged to learn through many centuries of discovery and refinement.

When our modern parent was moved to wonder and reverence at the beauty of the sunrise ("How beautiful God's world is!"), her affirmation was accompanied by an understanding of the world that identified several natural processes that explained what she was seeing. We would not suggest that her refined scientific understanding of these processes increased the truth (authenticity) of her affirmation, but only that her affirmation is accompanied by the scientific understanding that she has.

As long as this relationship between scientific descriptions of the world and religious affirmations about the world is kept clear—where affirmations are like persons and descriptions are like the clothing they wear—there will be no problem between religion and science. The problem arises when the truth of a religious affirmation is made to depend on the accuracy of the scientific understanding that accompanies it.

Let's illustrate this point with one other example drawn from personal life: When a couple gets married, they bring with them a commitment to a relationship that they hope and assume will be a lifetime one. Their relationship is as authentic (true) as it can be. They also bring with them their own understandings of marriage and of each other's mind and personality. Their relationship is accompanied by certain understandings based on their experience with each other so far.

As the couple journeys together through time and experience the various challenges that life brings, their relationship matures. Their understandings of marriage and of each other are no doubt refined, perhaps even changed significantly in some ways. The ideas and beliefs that accompany maturing relationships naturally experience modification as life provides the means for refining them, and the healthy relationships will "put on the clothes" of the new understandings that reflect a more accurate grasp of the reality of the world the relationship lives in.

Religious faith always expresses itself and understands itself in terms of the world where it finds itself, and the worldview (the understanding of the world that is generally accepted as accurate) of its time becomes the "clothing" it wears. Think about what happens when some discovery or development of experience occurs that alters the way people understand their world. Religious faith can either re-clothe itself in the new and more accurate understanding of the world, or it can defend the accuracy of the previous understanding of the world and make accepting its truth (accuracy) a condition of being faithful.

To illustrate this point, look at an historical example that demonstrates how easy it is to forget these basic principles.

A Case Study: Galileo and the Church

In the seventeenth century, Galileo popularized the findings of Nicholaus Copernicus from almost a century earlier that challenged the geocentric view of the world. This earlier theory that the earth was the center of the world and that the heavenly bodies revolved around it, based on the work of Aristotle and Ptolemy, had been embraced for 1500 years. Everything the church taught about the Christian faith was accompanied by this worldview, and it was assumed to be an essential part of theological truth.

When the theories of Copernicus were verified by Galileo's observations, this geocentric worldview was threatened by replacement with a heliocentric (sun-centered) worldview, thus calling into question the accuracy of the beliefs about the natural world that had been assumed for so long.

Galileo was tried before the Inquisition and condemned in 1633, after being forced to recant his findings and discoveries with regard to the structure of the solar system. He was placed under house arrest and ordered not to write or teach any more. The prohibition did not stop him, however. He continued to write and produced before his death other major works that were smuggled to Protestant Holland, where they were published.

In 1992 the Catholic Church finally officially admitted that it had erred in condemning Galileo, and subsequently embraced the role of science in an ongoing refinement of human understanding.

The Church with its power had slowed temporarily the advancement of what we now know as modern science, but it did not stop it. Others, like Isaac Newton, carried forward the refinement of a human understanding of the world; and the Church would no longer be the authority on matters of science, even though, with its diversified expressions after the Reformation, it has continued to try to be so.

A Final Word about Faith and Science

Perhaps the simplest way to put the essence of this part of our study is to say that religious thinking and scientific thinking are two different yet complementary and compatible ways of responding to ourselves and our world.

Every expression of religious faith (every religious affirmation) is accompanied by a particular understanding of the natural world (worldview). Scientific investigations and discoveries tend to change and refine our understandings of the natural world (always a process—never finished). Religious faith can either re-clothe itself in new understandings of the natural world (realizing that a person who changes clothes is still the same person), or it can defend the accuracy of an earlier understanding of the world (as in the Church's response to Galileo).

The unnecessary conflict between religion and science occurs when religion attempts on the basis of its faith to provide scientific descriptions of the natural world, or when science attempts on the basis of its investigations and discoveries to provide religious affirmations about the world. When each does its own work, and is respected by the other for doing so, the human quest for understanding and meaning is working as it should.

Application:
What stays locked if this key of faith and science is not used?

In everyday life this relationship between faith and science tends to become an issue where an emphasis in religious education is accompanied by an assumption that the Bible is "true" on both the level of its faith expression and the level of its factual accuracy in its accompanying understanding of the natural world. When a child has learned the stories of the Bible and absorbed the worldview of those who used those stories to communicate the meaning of their faith—for example, in creation and the structure of the universe—and then the child begins to learn in scientific studies a more modern understanding of the world, there is often the dilemma of whether to believe the Bible or the results of scientific investigation.

It has not been unusual in educational settings for there to be a supposed conflict between what is believed to be a biblically based understanding of creation and a scientifically supported concept of the evolution of life on the planet. Such conflicts will be less likely to occur if parents and children make careful use of this key that distinguishes between the scientific descriptions of the world and the religious affirmations about the world.

Key #8—
Faith and History

You will notice that our "keys" are becoming a little more complex than the ones with which we began. The arenas that remain locked without their embrace and use are not as easily identified and described as the earliest ones, but they become increasingly important as the process of theology moves in and about the various features of the faith relationship. The one we now consider deserves careful thinking and appropriation in faith's quest for understanding.

I have described this key as "faith and history" for the obvious reason that our faith tradition is historical in a number of ways. First, it is based upon and grows out of events and experiences that happened on the stage of history. The foundational experiences are specific and concrete, and while a long evolution in what they mean has characterized their development, there is little question that their roots are solidly in the soil of history.

Second, the faith tradition is historical in that its early and foundational formulations (testimonies) are conceived and expressed in the language and concepts of their time and place. They reflect the understandings of the natural world and of human experience that were current at their time. Whatever they say and point to about God's relation to the faith community and to the world in general employs not only the religious affirmations of their experience, but also their "worldview" descriptions of what they understood to be the nature of the world around them, as we discussed in our last section.

Third, our faith is historical in that a key element of its experience is rooted in engagement with life as it is lived on the world stage and in the human community. While its testimony clearly affirms that it is God who has acted to initiate the faith experience, and that the covenant relationship is "spiritual" in nature, it is not primarily an "other-worldly" faith that disconnects its participants from the everyday world of life.

To put the point simply, biblical/Christian faith is rooted in history, mediated through history, and lived in history.

Theology's quest for understanding encounters this historical feature of faith in our recognition that history is not simply the past, but is a kind of animated stage of three dimensions:

1. an accumulating past that serves to bring us to where we are
2. an ever-moving present that responds to that past and whose decisions determine the path forward
3. a future that is a guiding vision and a slate on which history's story will continue to be written

A theology of a faith that is historical, then, will be aware of and a steward of the past, responsibly engaged in the decisions of the present, and committed to a vision for the future. The late world religions scholar Huston Smith explained this perspective by describing the Zen of Buddhism: "Infinite gratitude toward all things past; infinite service to all things present; infinite responsibility to all things future."[5] This explanation suggests the way in which the three dimensions of history are recognized and embraced across faith traditions. Christian theology cannot let itself become exclusively attached to any one or two of these at the expense of the others.

Beyond this basic recognition of the interdependence of faith and history, the way in which the theological story is told reflects some of the complexity of how testimony and history interact. If the core of the testimony is, "Let us tell you how we have experienced God acting in our history, drawing us into a transforming covenant relationship that becomes the 'new lens' through which we see everything," the particular nature of that history becomes an integral part of the testimony. How that history is understood and how it is communicated become an essential part of the "package" of the religious affirmation.

We see this most pointedly in the older parts of the testimony, where the historical framework for God's engagement in history is beyond the scope of what we would consider normal historical study. The parts of our Old Testament that contain what we call the "pre-history" of Israel, and other earlier parts of the narrative of Israel's journey as a covenant people—where there is little if any of what we rely on to clarify historical contexts—leave us with a history that is quite different from what we have, for example, as the history of the Protestant Reformation or of the Great Awakening.[6]

The literary vehicles of the history that accompanies the theological content of these early affirmations of God's engagement with the covenant community have a distinctive quality about them that requires careful reflection and understanding. They are not the kind of data-supported, factual descriptions of a setting that can be cross-referenced and verified by appeals to evidence that stands in its own right as established fact. Rather, they are stories that focus more on meaning and values than on precise historical information, and working with this feature of them is often a challenge for people who have embraced a seamless historical fabric for the Bible and its testimony.

Before examining a few of the specific manifestations of this challenge, let's state briefly the "key" concept that is at work here: Faith (the "faith that seeks understanding") occurs in historical events and experiences, its understandings are framed in terms of that history, and its testimony is expressed in the concepts and language of that framework. But the authenticity of the faith experience is not the same as the historical context in which it occurs or in terms of which it is expressed. Put simply, it is like a heartfelt letter inside a historical envelope, the form and style of which might well change over time and place. The content of the letter is not identified with the color and shape of the envelope. This distinction is the key that we are working with here.

Now, let's look specifically at a few of the particular ways this distinction can show up in some challenges experienced in the community's theological work—the work of "everyday theologians."

In the prehistory that we find in the earliest chapters of Genesis, and in the narratives that pre-date the more contemporary historical records that developed with culture's advancements in writing and record keeping, we find several literary styles in the narrative that offer speculative and poetic "envelopes" for the covenant story.

To start with what is probably the most challenging of these styles when identified as part of the Bible, the literary vehicle of myth is the first we encounter. While the popular understanding of myth is often limited to "something that isn't true," we find upon a closer look that myths and mythology are ancient ways of expressing what lies beyond the realm of ordinary observation—what we would label as mystery. Specifically, it points to things affirmed about God (or the gods) that engage the world. Saying that the sun god drives his chariot across the sky on a daily basis is a mythological statement, and so is saying that the spirit of God brooded over the chaos of primeval waters before beginning the work of creation. Both are using poetic/mythological imagery to point to realities that are beyond what can be explained empirically.

To suggest that mythology is the literary vehicle of the early part of the biblical testimony is to deny neither its historicity or its truth, it is simply to recognize that this literary means of expression is the one best suited to frame the testimony's affirmation that the world as they (and we) know it is the result of God's creativity. Poetry and mythology are powerful tools for opening levels of truth that lie deeper than surface, factual accuracy. As theologian Marcus Borg has put it, while myths are not literally true, they are more than literally true.[7]

Moving from the prehistory of the earliest chapters of Genesis, we find that literary styles that point beyond themselves also figure in the narratives of Israel's covenant journey. With varied connections to "actual" history, legends, sagas, parables, and other creative forms of storytelling carry the narrative of the covenant journey forward toward an increasing measure of recorded history. These stories—even those that are the creative work of the community—are rooted in historical experience and portrayed as the community's "real" history, even as it shows marks of being fictionalized to emphasize the "truth" (i.e., meaning) they seek to convey.

A Particular Challenge for a Historical Faith and Its Theology

When theology begins to understand and express a faith experience that is rooted in particular historical events, in which God is believed to have acted in ways that have created and nurtured a faith community, it naturally derives theological meanings from those events. Something that occurs, such as an escape from bondage in Egypt, followed by a time in a wilderness journey, becomes in theological reflection the Exodus, the pivotal experience of the founding of the covenant community of Israel. The precise details of that event lie beyond the reach of historical investigation, but the story of its occurrence and the meaning that developed around it for Israel's covenant testimony are preserved in vivid form in the narrative that keeps its significance alive and well in Israel's life.

Other events follow a similar pattern throughout the biblical testimony, in both testaments, as the story of Israel's pilgrimage and the portraits of the life and ministry of Jesus portray and preserve the meaning and significance of what God has done with and through God's people.

The process that we see happening here, as historical events become the locus of an encounter between God and people that brings about a covenant partnership that is the foundation for an ongoing faith community, is something that we might call a process of "theologizing history." This somewhat awkward term seeks to point to a process of providing a spiritual overlay to some aspect of history that raises it from the surface of historical experience to make of it something of much greater significance. What might have been seen as an ordinary event to some is seen by this community's "eye of faith" as a much more "weighted" occurrence—one that has ultimate significance.

So far, so good: We can understand from our own experience how ordinary events, chance occurrences, and routine encounters can take on much greater significance when seen and understood in retrospect. We tend to "theologize" our own personal histories as we look back to see how certain parts of those histories play a larger-than-life role in our ongoing life stories.

Understanding a process of theologizing history is not hard when we realize how we tend to do that on many levels of thinking about our experiences. In theological work we do it quite easily as we remember and build our personal stories around experiences that become landmarks of our faith journeys.

The challenge for reflection and interpretation of a historical faith arises when this process gets reversed. Theologizing history occurs when a theological interpretation of an event or encounter lifts it from the surface of ordinary history (something that happened) to a level of religious/spiritual significance. What might have been a chance or routine conversation is later seen as a turning point in one's life.

Sometimes, in a person's testimony about that experience, it is difficult to tell where the actual event stops and the theological interpretation of its significance begins. Fortunately, we don't have to, because we recognize this process as the way a historical faith works. We see it both in our personal experience and throughout the testimony of the Bible.

The reverse of this process happens when instead of theologizing our history, we "historicize" our theology. This distinction is at work in a number of tensions that occur in biblical study and in theological reflection.

Let's go back to our observation that faith expressions (testimonies) are framed in understandings that are held by those who express them. The language, concepts, and recollections of events that are the framework of the testimony are essential parts of them. But, as we have noted, the authenticity/truth of the testimony is not tied to the framework in terms of which it is expressed, and we separate the meaning of the expression from the particular details of the setting. If an event in which a divine encounter is experienced is described in "larger than life" terms, we understand the emphasis to have a literary and theological purpose beyond historical descriptive precision.

If we were to reverse the process of theologizing our history and instead engage in a process of historicizing our theology, we would be using the significance of our theological meaning to solidify the historical framework in terms of which it has been expressed. Rather than building theological meaning from a particular event or experience (theologizing history), we would be creating history from the significance of our theological meaning (historicizing theology)

I hope this doesn't appear to be a playing of word games. I do believe it represents something that takes place in individual and community responses to the core testimony of a faith that is "historical." Perhaps we can best illustrate the point with a few examples from our core testimony.

Creation

Let's look first at the Bible's account(s) of creation in the book of Genesis. The familiar first chapter details a process of creation over a six-day period, moving from the most basic features of light and darkness, through the features of the planet, heavenly bodies, plant life, and the simple to most complex forms of animal life.

As we noted in our earlier discussion of the use of mythological language and imagery to speak of divine activity, this poetic introduction to the biblical testimony offers a beautiful and profound theological affirmation of the relation of creator to creature and creation. To the ancient minds of these ancestors in the faith (and in many ways also to our own), somehow, somewhere beyond the reach of human understanding the universe came into being; and, as they spoke of it, they pushed back into the mystery with an expression of the relationship that their faith gave them of the who, what, and why of the "beginning." The how, the when, and the where were part of their story, too, and that reflects where their understanding of the natural world was at their point in history.

Here is where we can see our distinction at work. They theologized the history by offering a theological affirmation of the creation as a relational act of a creator who established a partnership in and with creation and its creatures to carry the human journey forward. However, whenever and wherever it happened, its significance is to be found in its purpose and in the relationship that it established. That is history theologized.

If we were to reverse that process, to take the theological affirmation and its framework of its expression and historicize it, we would claim its framework as history in the sense that this is precisely what happened, just as described. Faith, then, would include not only an embrace of the theological affirmation of the relation of creator and creation, but also an acceptance of the framework of its expression as history—in the sense of a factual account of what happened.

The second chapter of Genesis offers a similar theological affirmation of a creative partnership between creator and creation, but within a different framework of the how, when, and where of the process of creation. Comparing the two shows how a theological affirmation can be made on the basis of different understandings of the history that is assumed.

In this account, the origin of the natural world is theologized into the relationship of covenant faith, even though the description of how it happened is set forth in quite different terms.

If that faith and its theology seek to historicize the assumptions of how the world began, we find it becoming a matter of faith to believe that God spoke the world into existence in six days, as in Genesis 1, or that the Lord created by the "hands-on" method described in Genesis 2.

The presence of these two accounts side by side in the canon of scripture perhaps should encourage us to see that theological affirmations can faithfully be accompanied by the wide range of historical understandings that evolve over the course of history. Making it a matter of faith to absolutize a particular historical framework (historicizing one's theology) leads to a focus that we might call "conceptual idolatry" (elevating certain historical understandings to ultimate status).

The Exodus

A second illustration of theologizing history and its opposite (historicizing theology) can be seen in the foundational narrative of the Exodus.

The testimony portrays the Exodus in highly dramatic and engaging form, with Moses as God's partner in a liberating work on behalf of God's people. The departure from Egypt and the beginning of the journey to the land of promise happened on the historical stage, but the story of that liberation and its place as the foundation of covenant faith rises to a point of extreme theological significance, well beyond the specific details of the historical event itself. The movie *The Ten Commandments* and other portrayals of the details of that liberation, departure, and escape create images of events that tend to historicize the theology of God's liberating work.

Joshua and the Sun Standing Still

Still another example that illustrates this distinction between theologizing history and historicizing theology is the familiar account of Joshua's prayer and the Lord's response of causing the sun to stand still in the heavens for a full day to allow the Israelites to prevail over the Amorites (Josh. 10:12-15).

The narrative portrays a memory of a victory over significant odds, and credits the additional time allowed by the stopping of the sun with that outcome. To the worldview of the time, a gift of extra time to accomplish a difficult task might well have employed the concept "time stood still for us." And, an image of the sun standing still at the command of God, in response to a general's prayer, is not hard to understand and is in perfect keeping with the cosmology of the time.

Whatever happened to enable the Israelites to be victorious, the narrative clearly theologizes it to testify that God was with them in their effort. If we reverse the process and historicize the theology of the testimony, we may find ourselves insisting, because it is Scripture, that the sun really did stand still for twenty-four hours, with all of the implications that that would raise for the functioning of the physical universe, as we understand it now. Requiring a belief in the truth of that as a historical fact and as a mark of faithfulness can become a major obstacle to modern minds' understanding of the meaning of this part of the testimony's invitation to see God at work in history.

Jonah and the Great Fish

The story of Jonah is an obvious illustration of the distinction between theologizing history and historicizing theology, since it has the marks of a fictionalized narrative to portray the experience of a reluctant prophet.

Jonah is called to go speak against the city of Nineveh, and he responds to that call by hopping on a boat going in the opposite direction to avoid the challenge. When a storm threatens the boat and all its occupants, and when Jonah's effort to escape from God's call is discovered, he is tossed overboard to curtail the risk He is swallowed by a big fish and remains in its belly for three days before being deposited back on shore to reconsider his decision to accept God's invitation. It is easy to understand that the narrative value of the "fish story" is making the message of the book memorable.

The story continues with other dramatic features, but the "fact" of his sojourn in the fish has often been the occasion of healthy questioning, especially for children who are being taught the Bible's truths. "Did that really happen?" is a question we have all heard (and raised) as we have thought about and taught this story of Jonah.

Since the story has more features of a parable than a historical report, it is easy to point to its meaning (its theology) at a deeper level than its history. Still, I can recall from days early in my ministry when a "test" of one's true faithfulness to the Bible was whether one believed that the fish part of the Jonah story was true on the factual level.

I don't mean to suggest that the position one might take on that question is a mark of one's faithfulness. But I do suggest that to take this very effective way of emphasizing the importance of responding to God's call and making of it an indisputable historical fact is an example of historicizing theology.

So, we conclude this longer section on the intimate relation of faith and history, having underscored its richness and complexity, where history is the foundation, the landscape, and the future arena of covenant faith's journey; and having pointed to at least one of the risks of making theological affirmations into historical facts.

The key of faith and history is an important one in the work of theology, on both the professional and the everyday level. Many tensions and conflicts within the family of faith can find their resolution in an understanding of this relationship.

Key #9—

Faith and Personal Development

As our study has progressed, our "key ring" of concepts that are basic to faith's quest for understanding has grown fuller with keys that have become a bit more complicated. This is because faith, as we have come to experience and understand it, is more complex and profound than a simple decision to believe certain things. As with relationships of other kinds, faith can have uncomplicated beginnings and is accessible by a wide variety of entry points. It might begin in a focused experience in a definite time and place, or it might come to life over a long period of absorption in the ethos of a community that lives by its precepts and commitments. In any case, faith is a part of our growth and development as persons, both individually and in our network of relationships.

This next key in the theological process opens a door to another dimension of our theological work. Up to now, we have been thinking about concepts and discernments that help us in our own refinement of our understanding of faith. But implied in everything that we have considered is the fact that the faith journey is a pilgrimage undertaken in the company of other pilgrims, whose theological work has helped shape our understanding, and whose ongoing path will be influenced by ours.

So, this key brings us to a dynamic in our collective faith experience that moves beyond our own path and invites us to give careful attention to the paths and places on those paths of others. It is an area of study that is more complex than a simple discernment of concepts (such as our earlier distinction between faith and beliefs, or the difference between the content of a testimony and the cultural language and concepts within which it is wrapped).

We have affirmed that the theologian's work—even that of the "everyday theologian"—involves not only one's own journey, but also a responsibility to participate in the nurture and growth of others with whom the journey is shared. The coin of theology has both a personal and a collective side.

This part of our work is closely related to what has developed over the past century as the field of developmental psychology. Many influential voices have brought this study to the work of educators, parents, and others who embrace the calling of providing leadership to growing persons. A vast body of literature has emerged from this work, and it is available in many places for those who wish to delve into it. Key names such as Jean Piaget and Erik Erikson will be familiar to those who have studied or worked in education and other related professions.

Application of the insights of developmental psychology has also emerged in the study of religious development. Pioneering studies by Lawrence Kohlberg and Gordon Allport have focused attention on moral development and on the maturation process that occurs in the religious dimension of life. A pivotal work bringing these insights specifically to the process of faith development is that of James Fowler, whose *Stages of Faith* [8] is a comprehensive description of the process by which a faith experience matures.

Most recently, theologian and author Brian McLaren has offered a current application of this way of thinking about faith in his *Faith after Doubt*,[9] a readable treatment of both the challenges and the possibilities along the path of faith's journey.

I mention these resources as available tools for broadening and deepening understanding of this arena of the theologian's task. And, I mention them with the suggestion that an important feature of the active part of theological work is understanding the place on the journey where one's companions are currently moving (or not moving) in order to be helpful to them.

A couple of years ago, after a minor shoulder injury from a fall, I was privileged to "enjoy" the services of an extremely competent physical therapist. He was highly qualified and knew a great deal about anatomy and the physiological functions of the body. With unlimited time, he could have probably remodeled me completely into a much better physical being; but in our circumstance, he spent a good deal of time watching my shoulder movement and listening to what I was experiencing as I tried to move it. He took measurements and made notes. Then and only then did he begin the process of applying his vast knowledge in a way that was focused on my specific need to move my tendons and muscles in the direction of healing. His knowledge needed a careful understanding of my need in order to be of help to me.

I mention this experience to suggest that a theological understanding of the faith relationship can be analogous to professional knowledge in other fields—it is a deeper understanding than might ordinarily be the case for many. That is not a cause for pride or a sense of superiority, but rather a simple recognition of a level of understanding that can be a source of help to others.

Just as my therapist's knowledge of physiology was a necessary component of his ability to help me, so was his willingness to work to understand just where I was in the physiological process before focusing and applying his knowledge to my case.

As noted at the beginning of this section, this key that examines faith and personal development is a heavier one than the other keys; in fact, it might deserve a fob of its own. Studying the developmental aspects of faith is a longer and more involved commitment than simple, conceptual refinements; but, for the everyday theologian, it is a worthy investment, as opportunities will present themselves in many contexts for "theological therapy" along the pilgrimage.

To begin, let's note a few observations about the analogy of human growth and development and of faith development. Consider the developmental stages of infancy; childhood; adolescence; and young, middle, and senior adulthood. We are familiar with the typical characteristics of each stage: the utter dependence and emerging awareness of infancy; the awe, energy, curiosity, and emerging independence of childhood; the awkwardness, uncertainty, hormonal turbulence, and increasing independence of adolescence; the early responsibilities of adulthood and the evolution of those responsibilities as vocation, family, and aspirations find their working relationships.

The suggestion is obvious from the foregoing that the faith experience follows a similar pattern to our physical, intellectual, and emotional development. It might, and often does, coincide with traditional developmental stages. Religious guidance focused on age-appropriate content for faith formation is carefully focused on the intellectual, emotional, and social development of children and adolescents, with the assumption that faith at those stages will function in harmony with other features.

But a person's religious experience does not always coincide with one's culturally generalized developmental process. The faith relationship, as we have been thinking about it here, can and does occur at any age and proceeds from that point forward—whatever that point is. Imagine the "new birth" of a transformational experience. Its earliest stage is characterized by an enthusiastic embrace of what it means at that point of the person's life, a dependence on the "parent" community or individual that has "midwifed" the birth, and a consuming focus of energy. It moves to rapid discovery of all the features of its new world, along with the affirmation and encouragement of "cheerleaders." It continues to mature into its own adolescence of making the transitions from the simpler understandings of what the faith means through the challenges of refinement in response to questions in the intersection of one's faith and the living of everyday life. There is an observable "adolescence" to a growing religious experience, no matter at what chronological age it happens to be. Critical thinking and questions about childhood beliefs seem to come naturally at this stage.

The "adult" stages of a maturing faith relationship can be identified and compared to the general features of adulthood. The transitions to, through, and beyond the responsibilities that accompany adult life have their theological correlates in the faith journey.

As a way of offering a helpful description of the qualities that characterize the direction of a growing faith, let's look at the features described by Gordon Allport as the characteristics of what he calls a "mature religious sentiment." [10] What follows is a brief description of these features. A mature faith, he says, will be:

- *Well-differentiated*: It will be recognized for its complexity and understood in terms of its relationship to other parts of life and thought. An "undifferentiated" faith will typically be lacking in critical thought, one-dimensional in its understanding, and simplistic in its acceptance of traditional teachings. This is strictly a description of understanding, not an evaluation of the authenticity of one's devotion.

- *Both derivative and dynamic*: It is rooted in a tradition that gives it its basic framework, yet embraces the autonomy of experiential integrity that can claim its own authority for an ongoing life transformation. It is both respectful toward that from which it has come, but also open to that which it is becoming.

- *Productive of a consistent morality*: "… an immature [faith] is very likely to raise moral storms, and sporadically alter conduct, [but] it lacks the steady, persistent influence of the seasoned religious outlook."[11] A passionate response to specific issues becomes part of a larger framework of moral concern.

- *Comprehensive*: It involves growth toward a holistic framework for life and commitment, embracing a larger reality than that of particular experience. "The religion of maturity makes the affirmation 'God is,' but only the religion of immaturity will insist, 'God is precisely what I say He is.' The Hindu Vedas were speaking mature language when they asserted, 'Truth is one; men call it by many names.'"[12]

- *Integral*: It will move toward connecting one's faith to the larger framework of life, which includes the several other dimensions of experience—the scientific, the economic, the political. The greatest challenge to this feature is how one's faith responds to the problem of evil and the suffering of innocent persons.

- *Heuristic*: It will recognize the lack of guarantees of certainty in the realm of faith. Confidence is distinct from certainty: "It is characteristic of the mature mind that it can act whole-heartedly even without absolute certainty. It can be sure without being cocksure." [13]

As we noted earlier, these features are descriptive of a growing process and are not meant to be evaluations of the authenticity of one's faith. As a part of life, a faith relationship is a journey from less mature to more mature understandings, and is thus in itself a theological exercise (faith seeking understanding). Everyday theologians participate in this process in two ways: monitoring one's own progress in the journey and assisting others in theirs. Understanding the stages and the directions of that maturation is key to both tasks.

This means that in our caring for one another theologically we need to be able to discern where a companion is on the developmental journey in order to know how best to offer what we have in the way of shared experience. Becoming as knowledgeable as possible is not the same as becoming an expert, but it is a prerequisite to being a faithful steward of the fruit of one's own quest for understanding.

As a specific suggestion, I would propose a careful reading of the earlier mentioned book by Brian McLaren, *Faith After Doubt*, especially his delineation of the four stages of the faith pilgrimage, as a way of understanding and respecting the places on the pilgrimage where we and our companions find ourselves.

Key #10—
Faith and Other Faiths

This final key of personal discernment on our key chain of conceptual tools for engaging in the work of theology as faith seeking understanding involves a feature of our faith journey that has come into increasing focus in recent years. The globalization of our personal awareness and the increasing experiences of intercultural relationships have broadened and deepened many aspects of life.

The impact of this process has had an effect on how we think about and interpret our own religious faith as well, as encounters with other faiths have become more personal and more frequent.

This key invites us to give some careful attention to the relationship of the faith that is the core of our understanding of life and the faith of others that serves the same function for them. In short: How does my Christian faith—which I embrace as the "way, the truth, and the life" (John 14:6)—relate to the faith of my Muslim or Hindu neighbor or co-worker, who lives by and with a similar, yet different, commitment?

This question requires some careful re-thinking of what has been in many quarters a traditional understanding of the uniqueness and supremacy of Christian faith over all others. In varying degrees, an assumption that Christian faith is the only "real true" faith and others are at varying levels of inferiority to it has been an underlying premise of faith's reflection and understanding.

This assumption, growing out of the profound transformation that God's disclosure of a grace-based faith relationship has had on its recipients, is quite understandable. From our first Christian theologian and writer, the Apostle Paul, and throughout Christian history, the passion to "spread the word" has fueled the missionary spirit of the Christian movement. "Winning the lost," working to "bring others to Christ," and many other calls to Christian evangelism have encouraged noble and at times heroic efforts to extend the "good news" to the world.

In working with students over the years as this question has become more frequent, two needs emerged for us as we sought to broaden and deepen our understanding of faith in an increasingly pluralistic religious context.

The first need has been simply to become more informed about the faith traditions that we find accompanying our fellow pilgrims along life's journey. The popularity of courses in comparative religions testifies to an increasing level of interest in the faith traditions of others, and a broadening of knowledge that naturally arises from intercultural encounters on both personal and community levels is a significant part of the process of being informed.

The second need emerges when this new knowledge leads one to raise questions about the assumptions that have been held and perhaps unquestioned about the "truth" (or lack of it) of the faiths of others. The need here is not only for knowledge of the faith of others, but also for a clarification of one's perspective toward that other faith. It is to this second need that this key will respond. We will begin by describing several optional frameworks that offer ways of thinking about the question.

An Exclusivist Perspective

Approaching faith with an exclusivist perspective tends to draw a clear line between the truth that has been experienced and everything else. It can be broadly focused to include all the differences within the Christian family, or it can be narrowly focused to claim truth for only one part of that family (identified by sect or denomination). Its mark is its understanding that there is one clear and unmistakable way to be truly faithful, and other ways are not. A key biblical verse in support of an exclusive perspective is the above noted John 14:6 (Jesus saying, "I am the way, the truth, and the life—no one comes to the Father except through me").

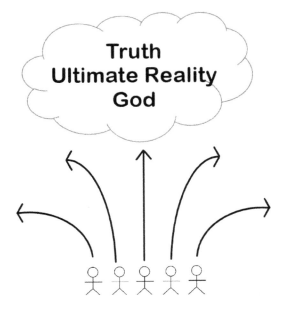

The perspective of exclusivism, in both its "hard' and "soft" forms, has been a part of the Christian pilgrimage through history. Its strength lies in the clear focus of its devotion. Its weakness lies in its exclusion of ways of being faithful that do not conform to the frame-work of its particular experience. "Our way is the only way" would be its mantra, and it fuels not only the spiritual security of personal certainty, but also the missionary spirit that courageously seeks to "bring others into the fold." Its hard form suggests, "We have the truth—too bad for you." Its soft form appeals, "Here is the truth, and we want very much for you to have it, and we will go to great, even sacrificial lengths, to make that so."

A Relativist Perspective

Opposite to an exclusivist perspective is that of relativism. As the label implies, this perspective would see all ways of being faithful as expressions of personal and cultural differences that lead to different ways of believing and behaving in response to the religious dimension of life. Examples are drawn from primitive cultures and from the vast array of religious traditions that have developed throughout history as evidence that there cannot be "one true way" of being religious that excludes all others.

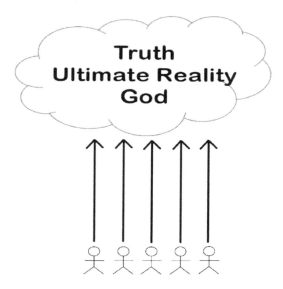

Defined by its complete open-endedness, its strength lies in its recognition of the plurality of ways of being religious—no way excluded, no way preferred. Its weakness lies in its lack of any clear criteria for assessing the relative value of any given perspective or tradition (one way is as good as another). Its popular mantra might be: "It doesn't matter what you believe, as long as you're sincere."

A Modified Relativist Perspective

Moving away from a purely relativist view on the perspective spectrum, we find an embrace of openness but a belief that there are differences that matter in terms of what a perspective stands for and how it works in history. While being open to the idea that "all roads lead to Rome," there are some roads that get there more effectively and with less chance of getting lost or taking a wrong turn. Much like an approach to town from an outlying neighborhood, there are surface streets with various options and risks of wrong turns, and there are avenues and perhaps expressways that are more direct and easier to follow.

Flannery O'Conner's story title, "Everything That Rises Must Converge," is an image that captures this perspective of modified relativism: spiritual paths eventually find their common focus, but some find it more quickly, and not everything rises.

The modified relativist perspective tempers the strengths and weaknesses of exclusivism and relativism in a way that allows for passionate focus while at the same time allowing for corresponding passion and commitment within the framework of another faith. Its weakness lies in the arbitrariness that can be involved in the value criteria for assessing the relative truth of a given path.

A Partialist Perspective

Many years ago in an introduction to religion class, where we were discussing the various perspectives about the relationship of parts of a pluralistic religious world, a student offered a different image than the "roadway" one I was using to illustrate the options. She suggested that, rather than roads to a destination called "Truth," "God," or "ultimate reality," we might think of it as something that is viewed through the windows of various vantage points (i.e., religious traditions). Each view has its own "true" perception of the larger reality of Truth. Some "windows" offer a wider and perhaps clearer focused view of it. Some may overlap with the views from other windows, with shared images of the Truth. Some might be extremely narrow and limited in the portion of Truth that is seen. But all, even with these variances, still see "Truth."

But the one thing that could be said of all the windows is that no one offered a view of the whole of Truth. Some might see enough of Truth to speculate on what the rest of it looks like, but no one window enabled all of it to be seen directly.

Over the years, this image of a perspective toward the many faiths that now are part of the religious landscape has been a helpful one for me and for students and others who have sought to be faithful to our own experience and respectful and open to the faith experiences of others. It draws upon our Key #3 that encourages us to understand the "partiality of all our understandings" as we move toward greater maturity and refined understanding of the aspects of life, from the simple to the most complex.

To claim "partiality" for an understanding of one's faith is not to compromise its truth and value as the core of one's life. It is, rather, an honest recognition that the mystery toward which our faith points us is more complex and profound than any perception at a given time can grasp completely. Our own experience of growth in the faith journey offers plenty of examples of how this principle works: every stage is a process of refinement of our understanding of that relationship.

The principle of partiality does, however, protect us from the tendency toward thinking that what we know and have experienced as true is all there is to truth. Religious devotion seems particularly vulnerable to this tendency, because its significance is so profound in its meaning for its adherents, it is hard to imagine any other way that could be as true.

I have mentioned these perspective options and elaborated at some length on the last one because these represent the broad ways that the relationship of one's faith to other faiths can be understood. It is also the case that over the course of the faith journey, one's perspective on this relationship can and often does evolve in the direction of becoming more inclusive rather than exclusive, more partial than assuming complete understanding, more open to gaining insights from the faith of others, and a journey characterized more by cooperation and mutual enrichment than by competitiveness. It offers motivation and fuel for a trajectory toward community that crosses the lines of limited perception in a broadened quest for understanding that is an open frontier for theological thought and discovery.

The key related to understanding and acknowledging the truth of other faiths is in the early stages of its widespread use in the larger realm of theological work, especially among everyday theologians. Its seeds have been germinating for a long time in the work of formal theologians; but the increasing plurality of religious experience in the contexts where most people live, work, and worship is proving to provide fertile soil for their growth.

Notes

[1] Marcus Borg, *Reading the Bible Again for the First Time* (New York: Harper Collins, 2001).

[2] Shirley Guthrie, *Christian Doctrine*, rev. ed. (Louisville: Westminster/John Knox Press, 1994), 20-35.

[3] Howard Clinebell, *The Mental Health Ministry of the Local Church* (Nashville: Abingdon Press, 1965), 30-54.

[4] Ibid, 54.

[5] Huston Smith, interview with journalist Bill Moyers, April 23, 1996, https://billmoyers.com/content/a-personal-philosophy-the-wisdom-of-faith-with-huston-smith/.

[6] The reference here to the "pre-history and earlier parts of the narrative" is to Genesis 1–11 and to the patriarchal narratives of Genesis 12–50.

[7] Borg, *Reading*, 41, 62, 71

[8] James Fowler, *Stages of Faith* (New York: Harper and Row, 1981).

[9] Brian McLaren, *Faith After Doubt* (New York: St. Martin's Press, 2021).

[10] For an extended and helpful discussion of these features, see Gordon Allport, *The Individual and His Religion* (New York: The Macmillan Co., 1950), 59-83.

[11] Ibid., 74.

[12] Ibid., 78.

[13] Ibid., 81.

Part 2

Using the Keys to
Unlock Understanding

Helping Others Unlock Access to Understanding

The first part of our study focused on the personal concepts and discernments that contribute to a fruitful engagement in the task of faith seeking understanding. The epistemological keys are largely ways of thinking that unlock helpful understandings of faith's vocabulary and resources. These ways of thinking will continue to be refined as the theological journey proceeds.

A second layer of being an everyday theologian emerges from one's experience as part of a community of fellow pilgrims on the quest for understanding. We have already reflected on how the experience of others has an important formative effect on how we understand our faith. Now we focus on the role we will play in the formation of others' understanding.

Our focus thus far has been on the opportunity, challenge, and responsibility of being a "thinking theologian"—in contrast to being a passive and unreflecting one, simply thinking and speaking in the formulas that have become habits from acceptance and repetition. Refining our understandings of faith and its relation to beliefs, the Bible, history, and scientific understandings of the world is an important process in the quest to have an understanding of faith that will encourage a good and helpful stewardship of the gift the faith relationship is.

As we have thought about this process and considered the contribution our faith community has made to our growth and nurture in faith, we have realized that faith is something of a "family affair," in the sense that we begin to experience faith in the context of a spiritually caring community long before we develop theoretical understandings of what it means. Similar to the love we experience much earlier than we develop concepts of love, faith is experiential before it becomes theoretical in formal theological concepts.

Faithful stewardship of that personal faith-family heritage involves a recognition of its contribution and an awareness of its influence in our formative thinking about what our faith means. Many believers grow beyond the specifics of that heritage as the horizons of life broaden to include realities that were not part of that particular context, but most retain something of the perspectives, the values, and the beliefs of that earlier experience. Gratitude for the care of one's formative family of faith, even when some of its features are adjusted to express more accurately what one's faith has come to mean, is a mark of faithful maturity and wisdom.

This recognition leads to the focus of this next section of our work with the "keys for everyday theologians." Having embraced our awareness of the faith family's contribution to our own journey, we naturally notice the opportunity and responsibility we have to be part of that contribution to those who are following us on the pilgrimage. So, this section will invite us to embrace the responsibility of being not only a "thinking theologian," but also a "practicing theologian."

The easy analogy here is that of persons who enter the professional fields of law and medicine. Study and refinement of the content of those fields and the concepts and perspectives that are essential to them is a long and arduous process, and one that is considered prerequisite to working in the field. The study, however, as essential as it is, is not an end in itself, but becomes the basis for the actual "practice" of law or medicine, as the knowledge and tools gained in one's study are put to use in the service of the community.

For everyday theologians, the process is not quite so formal, but the features of it are similar. While the "formal" theologians in the community's life get to do the heavy theological lifting—providing worship leadership and educational guidance, responding to the pastoral care questions and the crisis-induced spiritual struggles that come with living—the everyday theologians in the faith community have more influence than many realize, I believe, in the way their fellow pilgrims understand and grow in their faith. Peer influence (i.e., everyday education) may have more to do with shaping the understandings of faith and its components than formal pronouncements and official denominational positions.

For a number of years, I enjoyed and benefited from the leadership of a remarkable dean who frequently reminded us teachers, "We teach by everything we do and say"—meaning, of course, that education is not limited to the formal curriculum or what happens in the classroom. The way we treated students and each other, and the attitudes we reflected about the larger framework of school and community citizenship, and our general model of lifelong learning were all a part, in her mind, of what education was about. I believe she was right.

Everyday theologians may be the most effective teachers in the process of faith seeking understanding. Just as the choice is not whether to be a theologian, but what kind of theologian to be, so the choice is not whether to be a practicing theologian, but what kind of influence will my practice of theology have on those who travel with me. Will I offer a model of one who is "saved and satisfied," with little or no thought beyond the habitual formulas of familiar religious language? Or, will I be an example of one whose faith leads to openness and discovery of the depths of what the faith relationship means?

On the assumption that the second answer to the question is the more faithful one, let's think about how our "keys" might operate in the give-and-take of everyday theology. Let's also remember that anytime we think and speak about the various dimensions of our faith—God, how we know God, Jesus, the Bible and its truths, the church, ourselves as children of God, the future and destiny of history—we are engaging in theology.

Theology becomes formalized into several areas that correspond to the questions that naturally arise in the faith relationship. When a person of faith thinks about what God is like, those thoughts are concepts of God that in the faith community eventually become what is known as the doctrine of God. The question of who Jesus Christ is becomes what is called "Christology." Who we are in the faith relationship becomes the Christian understanding of what it means to be human (in traditional, pre-gender awareness theological works, this was known as the Christian doctrine of man). The nature of the faith community itself—what and who it is, its distinctive character—becomes a doctrine of the church, or "ecclesiology." The direction and destiny of history—how is God's reign over what happens in history will be fulfilled—becomes a doctrine of "last things," or eschatology.

Interpretations of these theological areas of thought become quite expansive and make up a vast volume of literature that is the substance of formal theology. As we noted in the introduction, this volume can be daunting and discouraging to the everyday theologian, just as the volume of legal and medical literature would be overwhelming to the everyday consumer of legal and medical knowledge and services. Still, the client and the patient are bona fide partners in the legal and medical dimensions of life.

In a similar way, the theological questions that occur in the normal process of life are authentic and deserving of careful attention and development, even if they do not lead to more formal volumes of interpretation. Their development is lived out in the growing understanding that occurs in the faith community. The need for commitment and care in their refinement is no less important than the more formal work that is produced in church and academy.

As a way of considering how our keys can be used to help others in their own theological thinking (and as a way of seeing ourselves as practicing theologians), I want to suggest that we consider some questions, statements, and issues that often arise in the course of the personal faith journey. And, as a way of connecting them to the traditional framework of theological reflection, I want to suggest too that we begin by arranging them around the traditional areas noted above.

What kind of God is this?

Let's consider a friend who has just begun to attend a Bible study as part of a renewed interest in the church and a desire to get more involved. She shares in conversation: "I am puzzled by the seemingly cruel and judgmental, even violent God of the Old Testament and the loving and compassionate God of the New Testament. How can this be, since the Bible is supposed to be true throughout? Does God change from one time in history to another?"

Think about which of our keys are in play here in this person's very sincere and reasonable question. Much of what she hears in her Bible study and in other church teachings emphasizes the trustworthiness of the Bible and the unchanging nature of God; so there is an understandable question in her mind about the different ways that God is portrayed.

The practicing theologian will not be too quick to offer an answer or solution. Like a lawyer who listens carefully to a client's concern or a physician who pays close attention to a patient's experience with symptoms, the practicing theologian will listen carefully to the question, not to give it an answer, but to help redirect it in a direction that will increase understanding of what lies beneath its surface.

A good beginning is to affirm the value of the question itself and to commend the discernment that has brought it to the surface. It is not the result of casual observation, but of some careful study of at least parts of the Bible and of some thinking about what God is like.

Obviously, the theological topic areas of the question have to do with the nature of God and the nature of the Bible; and they deserve more than a quick and satisfying response. In fact, the goal of theological guidance is not to satisfy but to encourage a bit of dissatisfaction in order to prompt deeper thinking and investigation.

As we think about a response to the question regarding "two Gods of the Bible" that will be refined by the keys we have developed, let's consider first what our own first experience with this question has most likely been. We may remember when this discovery first came to our awareness and the answers that may have been given to us at the time. How do we answer that question now, and what insights or discoveries have brought us to our current thinking on it?

At first, our friend's question seems to have to do with what God is like, and what is being experienced as a conflict between two concepts of God: (1) a powerful, judgmental, and at times cruel deity quick to punish wrongdoing and (2) a compassionate, forgiving, even sacrificially suffering God as revealed in the life and teachings of Jesus. Is God really like that, or like this?

One of the keys in play with this concern is Key #3 that points to the difference between a "reality" and our "concepts" of that reality. When we think or say things about God, we are giving thought and expression to our concept of God, and (most of the time) we realize that there is more to God than what our concept of God can embrace. The easy-to-recognize illustration of this distinction appears when we think about how our concepts of God have changed over time and experience in the journey of faith.

A closer look suggests that an important issue in the question has to do not only with the character of God but also with the consistency of the Bible and the appearance that it contradicts itself in its portrayal of God. Here we find a common challenge in communities of faith that emphasize the authority of the Bible and its trustworthiness as the "Word of God" to be true in all ways that pertain to faith.

So, two more keys come into play in our thinking with our friend on this question. Key #4 has to do with clarity about the nature of the Bible, and Key #6 invites us to think about what it means to affirm that the Bible is "true."

Let's look first at Key #4 that points to the importance of carefully refining our concept of what the Bible is (as distinct from what we affirm about its value and meaning). If we recognize it as a collective testimony of a community of people, developed over centuries of their experience as a covenant people with a God who has acted in decisive ways in their history, we are not surprised to find that it reflects generations of experience and understanding of who that God is and how that God has acted on their behalf.

The earliest expressions of their testimony will likely reflect a concept of God that in ways will be similar to the "gods" of their cultural setting. Over time, and through their experience in seeking to live the covenant relationship, that concept of God will likely be refined more specifically in terms of what that relationship comes to mean. So, the God who "behaves like the other gods" will become in their experience a God who is characterized more by the qualities of the relationship that the covenant embodies.

An early part of the testimony that portrays God ordering and taking delight in the slaughter of enemies, or as an arbitrary wielder of power, or as a cruel punisher of disobedience yields in later parts of the testimony to an image of God who reflects compassion, even to the point of suffering and self-sacrifice.

Understanding the Bible as testimony thus helps us see that these differences reflect not a God who is changing, but a process by which a people's concept of God is changing and growing toward a God who continues to be disclosed in the relationship of a covenant.

So, a first step in helping our friend who is dealing with this very understandable question is to suggest some careful thinking about the Bible as a "developing expression of the concepts of God that accompany an inspired people's faith journey."

This does not suggest that the Bible is less "inspired" than she thought it was. Rather, it shifts the understanding of "inspired" a bit from thinking of it as an "inspired text" to thinking of it as a "text offered by many generations of an inspired people," who embrace as part of the Bible's sacredness not only what it points to but also the process of their own growth of understanding in the covenant relationship. This is a key distinction in the concept of inspiration when applied to the Bible.

A possible follow-up question in our conversation with our friend might go something like this: "But how can the Bible be true and completely trustworthy as a guide for our lives if it contains such different ideas that are not really compatible with each other?"

Here our Key #6 helps us as we think with our friend about the "truth" of the Bible. Of course, our faith affirms as a basic theological principle the authority of Scripture as a guide and standard for evaluating truth claims that arise in faith's quest for understanding. But we don't study the Bible long before we run into things that raise the question of its truth. From relatively simple things such as who discovered the empty tomb on Easter morning and the descriptions of the process of creation in Genesis 1 and 2, to events that—told as they are from an ancient point of view—strain the mind and appear to be impossible exaggeration (such as the age of Methuselah, the sun stopping in they sky for a while to help Joshua win a battle, or Jonah's three days in the belly of a fish).

Our key that reminds us that there are levels of truth in the way we think and express ourselves can be helpful here, as we suggest perhaps that the truth of Jesus' parables and of some Old Testament stories may not lie in whether or not such a circumstance actually happened, but in the message or point the illustrations are offering to listeners. The truth of a parable lies at a deeper level than the level of factual accuracy.

So, a question to continue the thinking introduced by the use of this key is not so much the natural early question, "Is this true?" (as in, "Did this really happen like this?"), but "What kind of truth do we find in this part of the testimony?" Once we use this key to change the direction of the question, we are set to continue to probe the parable or other parts of the narrative for deeper meaning.

We will find this key at work in other questions that arise in our efforts to assist fellow pilgrims in their quest for faith's understanding. Here we can simply recognize, and help others to recognize, that much of the truth of the Bible lies at a deeper level than its surface.

So, a friend's seemingly simple question has begun a conversation that will likely continue, with at least a sense on her part that her question is important and worthwhile, and will open a doorway to a new level of understanding the Bible and the concepts of God it portrays. Entering that doorway invites discoveries still waiting to be found.

How can I know what to believe?

Sabrina grew up in a small city where church life was a normal part of community life. There were churches of several denominations, in addition to a small synagogue and recently a new mosque. She remembers enjoying Sunday school and the stories from the Bible that her teachers helped her learn. The events and characters of those stories—Adam and Eve in the Garden, Moses in the bulrushes, the children of Israel escaping from Egyptian bondage and meeting God in a special way in the wilderness, the conquest of the promised land, King David with his beautiful poems, and King Solomon and his wisdom—these became part of the fabric of who she was. Of course, the stories of Jesus and his disciples and Paul and his missionary journeys were part of that experience, too.

Her exposure through the care of this church community naturally enabled the biblical narrative to become a part of her framework for thinking about her religious faith. She was part of that story, because everything she was taught encouraged her to see this story as her story, too.

Even when she left home to get married, start a family and enter this new stage of her life journey, and even though her church involvement became less active with her change of location and new responsibilities, she held on to what she remembered as the biblical story as a kind of foundational narrative for her life and values. The lessons attached to the stories she had learned guided her decisions and relationships in a healthy way.

After a few years, she and her family connected with a church nearby at the invitation of a neighbor who was involved there and who thought her friends would enjoy the fellowship, Bible study opportunities, and children's activities and programs. Soon she found herself in a Bible study group made up of adults of varied backgrounds who were working through a kind of general introduction to the Bible—with attention given to its content, context, and major themes.

The leader of the group was not one of the ministers, but a layperson who had been a teacher in the church for a number of years, and who enjoyed facilitating groups such as this one in the process of deepening an understanding of the Bible. She was/is a good example of one of our everyday theologians.

During the course of the study, several members of the group raised questions about how to understand certain parts of the Bible, for example: whether Adam and Eve were the first human beings and whether some of the familiar stories might have been literary creations to convey and make memorable the spiritual truths they sought to convey.

It had never occurred to Sabrina to ask those kinds of questions. At first they were a little troubling, because they challenged some of the assumptions she had held about the Bible and its stories.

The teacher was careful to affirm the importance of the questions, and she pointed out the various ways that parts of the Bible can be understood. There are times, she said, when a particular part of the narrative seems to be intended as a more symbolic than literal expression, pointing to a truth that is more general than the specifics of the story.

That made sense to Sabrina, but she was still a bit troubled by the difference between what she had been taught and what she was now confronting as an alternative way of understanding parts of the Bible.

After a time, Sabrina mustered the courage to speak up and share her concern. "What do you do," she asked, "when your background and community tell you that you are supposed to believe something, and your own experience leads you toward believing something else?"

Hers is a perennial question shared by many Christians, who find that the belief frameworks of tradition or of personal background no longer fit the discoveries in the course of life and study There is a kind of unsettling "authority conflict" when the ideas and ways of thinking of one's tradition—either personal or formal in the sense of "official" beliefs—are confronted by the implications of new discoveries, either from the outside or from the inside.

The leader and members of Sabrina's Bible study group responded to Sabrina with various forms of gentle affirmation of her question, suggesting that she has given good expression to their own experience, and offering examples of how their beliefs have changed over the course of their faith journey. They were careful to encourage deep appreciation for the foundations laid by earlier experience, pointing out that faith calls one not to limit oneself to the foundation but to build upon it. Their responses have given Sabrina a basis for continuing to think about the relation of her faith and her beliefs (Key #2), and she will soon be joining them in that kind of help to others.

Do I have to believe this Trinity thing?

You have a co-worker who has recently become a part of a church fellowship that has been a welcome experience of new community for him. His lack of church involvement before has not been a problem, because a number of other people in the fellowship share a similar history. The emphasis is on inclusion and fellowship and discovery of ways to put their faith into action in their daily lives. He has spoken before of his enjoyment being part of this group.

At lunch one day this co-worker reports that he had experienced a rather confusing Bible study lesson that focused on the doctrine of the Trinity. The leader of the study suggested that this is an essential belief for Christians, and that the "God is one/God is three" concept is something that has to be accepted "on faith" even though it is hard to understand. The discussion left him more confused than inspired, and it seemed like an unnecessary trapping on an otherwise simple faith. As he put it, insisting that a Christian believe this concept seemed like insisting that one wear a tie to be fully dressed.

It's not hard to imagine this hypothetical scenario, and it's not hard to imagine his confusion.

How would you diagnose this person's theological need? Which of the keys are needed to help him respond to this confusion in a helpful and faithful way?

As we think about how we would try to respond, let's think about our own early encounter with the concept and doctrine of the Trinity. How did we react to it? What might have been helpful as we sought to understand it and its significance?

We would likely respond to our friend's concern with Key #1 (the relationship of faith and theology), with Key #2 (the relationship of faith and beliefs) a second and close one.

Before applying the keys directly to his question, we would want to affirm the Bible study leader's effort to describe this doctrine that has been a central one for theological understanding since the early centuries of the church's life. It is good to be aware of how the Christian community has understood the God with whom the faith relationship is engaged, and this is one central example of this understanding.

Since faith is the relationship our friend is experiencing, and since the doctrine of the Trinity is theology, some conversation about the relation of faith and theology would seem to be a good starting point.

As the early generations of the followers of Jesus processed the faith that had transformed their lives, they sought to find ways of describing what that faith meant and how they might help their children and generations that would follow them to think and speak meaningfully about their experience. They had experienced God as Creator and as a reality that provided order to the universe, and also as a covenant maker with their ancestors in the faith. They had experienced God in Jesus, through whom they had experienced God in a specific and transformative way. They had experienced God in a sense of God's presence with them in daily life as individuals and as a community. This one God had been experienced in different ways, much in the same way that one person can be experienced as a parent, a spouse, a sibling, and a friend (among other less direct relationships).

The early followers of Jesus came to think and speak of these diverse relationships in terms of three images: (1) Father, an image with deep roots in their heritage; (2) Son, drawing on the concept in the Gospels that spoke of Jesus as the Son of God; and (3) Spirit, which was a ready image, also with deep roots in their tradition, to point to the mysterious presence that accompanied them on their ongoing journey. These images gradually came to be a kind of official expression of how the one God could be experienced in different and distinct ways.

This is how the doctrine of the Trinity came to be. It was not something "revealed" that had to be believed, but instead was the result of a community's effort to speak meaningfully about what continued to be their experience with God. It was theology, and it was faith seeking understanding for themselves and for generations that would follow.

Now, to the specifics of our friend's question: Does one have to "believe in" the doctrine of the Trinity to have an authentic Christian faith experience? The short answer is no, in spite of what some traditions might require as a formal framework for membership and participation. It is helpful to understand what the doctrine is pointing to as the nature of God as experienced in the Christian context, but it is the nature of doctrine to be a pointer to faith's realities rather than being the object of faith's devotion.

Our first key helps us see and maintain the difference between faith and theology in contexts where the results of the latter can become substitutes for the substance of the former.

This leads to the relevance of Key #2 in thinking about our co-worker's question. Recall that every relationship is always accompanied by concepts and ideas that are the means of thinking about and communicating the meaning of the relationship. This is true of the relationship of faith, too, and those ideas and concepts are the beliefs that accompany it.

The doctrine of the Trinity—the belief that God is One/God is Three—is just that: a belief about what God is like. It gives expression to what is experienced as the unity and diversity of the mystery of God, and it has proved to be an effective way of pointing to and preserving a distinct feature of the Christian faith experience. While it has become part of Christian orthodoxy (official teaching), there have been those in the Christian family who have not embraced it as the preferred way of expressing their faith. Groups that may be familiar to our co-worker are the Church of Jesus Christ of Latter Day Saints, Jehovah's Witnesses, the Church of Christ, Scientist, and Unitarian Universalist Association.

Probably of more relevance to our co-worker's experience is the observation that even within a given pattern of beliefs about a relationship, there is likely to be some growth and change in those beliefs and the way they are understood, as time and experience do their refining work on how we understand things.

In the specific case of the doctrine of the Trinity, what first seems to be an unsolvable mathematical problem (1 = 3 and 3 = 1) becomes a way of seeing community as part of the nature of the divine reality we call God. If community is inherent in Godself, then humanity created in the image of God is also inherently community. This is a belief pattern that supports the emphasis we find throughout the Bible and Christian teaching on the importance of love of God and neighbor as the essence of faith.

So back to the original question: "Do I have to believe in this Trinity thing?" Its original short answer is still "No." But belief in the Trinity has proved to be a helpful way of affirming, pointing to, and preserving the distinctive nature of the Christian experience with God as both unified and diverse.

Key #2 involves a simple discernment: as faith grows, beliefs that accompany it change. Believing that there is both unity and diversity in the reality we call God is the basic meaning of this doctrine. But it invites us to new levels of meaning and belief as we see it as an invitation to think of God as a community of divine dimensions and as a community we are invited to join and participate in. We "believe in this Trinity thing" by embracing the community that it points to as the essence of godly life. Perhaps our conversation can help our co-worker to look forward to that.

How could Jesus be God and human at the same time?

Sarah does not remember not going to church. Her earliest memories recall the good times she had in Miss Dot's Sunday school class, where she learned the stories and sang the songs about Jesus. Those stories and songs have stayed with her through several years of other classes and choir experiences; and, without her realizing it, they have become a significant part of her personal "theology." She "took Jesus into her heart" at age 11, understanding that to mean she was making a commitment to live as Jesus would want her to live and to grow in that relationship going forward. She had plenty of help from her personal and church family in thinking about all that would mean, and she thrived in the happiness of this new level of her life.

Sarah is in her mid-teens now, still active in her youth group and developing the kinds of thinking that is typical of her age. She likes to ask questions, especially about things that are important to her. One evening in a youth group discussion she raised the question of how Jesus could be both God and a man at the same time.

Without realizing it, she was asking a question that occupied the early church for several centuries, as generations of the followers of Jesus engaged in what we now call the "Christological controversies." Different beliefs about the nature of the relationship of divine and human in Jesus the Christ sought to bring philosophical clarity to this seeming paradox of the Christian claim that "Jesus is Lord."

This is one of those areas of historical theology that strains the patience of those simply seeking help in understanding this central affirmation of the faith. Volumes of analysis are available that explore the content and implications of the various interpretations of the affirmation. (A brief and helpful summary is available in Coleman Ford's essay, "Christological Controversies in the Early Church," at www.thegospelcoalition. org.)

The outcome of this long process of discussion was essentially a return to two simple affirmations from the biblical testimony. The first can be seen in the gospel account of Simon's response to Jesus' question to the disciples regarding what people were saying about who he was: "Who do you say that I am?" Simon replied, "You are the Christ, the Son of the living God" (Matt. 16:16). And we see it in Paul's clear Christological affirmation: "God was in Christ, reconciling the world to himself … and entrusting the message of reconciliation to us" (2 Cor. 5:19).

The second biblical affirmation is woven throughout the testimony in various refrains to the Genesis 1 account that humankind is "made in the image of God" (vv. 26-27). The intimate communion of divine and human is part of the fabric of the covenant faith of the Bible. The most basic expressions of the church's Christology point to the mystery as well as the transparency of that mystery. Jesus is the normative disclosure of that mystery, and to follow him is to live into it.

This, of course, is a more detailed answer than Sarah wants or needs in response to her questions; but it is helpful to know that she is asking a question that has been a natural and understandable one throughout Christian history.

Our key again is #1—the relation of faith and theology. Faith asks questions, and theology offers answers in the form of interpretations that invite deeper thinking and more questions. Theology's answers can be helpful, sometimes even essential lenses through which faith can see the path of the journey, but embracing them is not a substitute for the journey itself. Theology is faith seeking understanding not faith having found a (final) understanding.

Again, applying the key to Sarah's question would involve commending her for raising a question that has been at the heart of the Christian tradition throughout its history and one that is an invitation to deeper thinking about living the life of a Jesus follower. Seeing the mystery of the divine/human relationship in Jesus opens the possibility of seeing that mystery in ourselves, in others, and indeed in the whole creation.

One further thought: our second key on the relation of faith and beliefs, is in play here. Faith in Jesus will naturally be accompanied by a variety of beliefs about Jesus, which will no doubt be modified and refined as the faith journey continues. Sarah can be reminded that things she has believed about Jesus may change with time, experience, and further study. This is a natural function of a maturing faith, and something to be welcomed as an ongoing gift of what she understands as the process of salvation.

How can the Bible be true when it contains so many inconsistencies?

We were about a month into our survey course on the Old Testament when Felix asked his question. We had looked at the two creation accounts in Genesis 1 and 2, the two versions of the flood narrative in Genesis 6–8, the two versions of the Israelites' escape from the Egyptians woven together in Exodus 14, and the two accounts of the occupation of the land of promise reflected in the books of Joshua and Judges.

We had just finished a consideration of the "pro-king" and the "anti-king" sources that appear in 1 Samuel 8–12, where the different perspectives on the establishment of a nation with a monarch are set forth. Felix, like anyone who looks carefully at this material, had a question that had been coming to the surface of his thinking. He had been conditioned by his experience to think of the Bible as an inspired and consistent record of what it describes, and this internal diversity was challenging that assumption with these divergent reports of events and perspectives.

His question was not an unusual one, and it illustrates the challenge that many students of the Bible face as their assumptions about it encounter what is actually there. A profound respect for and devotion to the Bible and its place in the faith community's life is often coupled with a concept of its sacredness that wraps a veneer of perfection around it that precludes inconsistency, historical or scientific inaccuracy, or other evidence of "imperfection."

In its public (and often weaponized) form, this assumption finds expression in claims of the "infallibility" or "inerrancy" of the Bible—concepts that discourage the kind of study that looks for deeper meaning in the text than what might be seen as surface truth.

Felix's question is essentially, "How can the Bible be true when there are so many inconsistencies in it?"

Everyday theologians experience this question in themselves and in others who share the faith journey. Let's think about how we might respond to Felix based on our keys: Which ones apply in this case, and how might we respond in a way that will encourage him to hold to his respect and devotion to Scripture, while at the same time deepening his understanding of these features of its testimony?

Remembering our Key #9—being careful to assess where our theological companion is in his maturing faith, and our role as an encourager of that process—we see that the primary area of theological concern has to do with the nature of the Bible as a key resource for the faith that seeks understanding (Key #4).

Felix is not upset or defensive in response to his discovery of the noted biblical inconsistencies; he is curious that he has never been encouraged to see them before and he wonders how an honest recognition of them can accompany a profound faith in the Bible as the "inspired Word of God." This suggests that he is ready to consider a refinement of his beliefs about the Bible that accompany his faith in the Bible (Key #2) as an important source for his faith journey.

Perhaps a good starting point would be the value of seeing the Bible as an evolving testimony of a people who have experienced God in their lives, which opens the door to a recognition that there will be many ways that testimony might express itself over time and in different contexts.

We of course would want to affirm Felix's question and its awareness of this feature of the biblical narrative. We might also share our own discovery of that feature of more than one version of some of the Bible's central stories: How did that come to our attention? What was our initial response to the discovery? What was helpful to us as we thought about it?

Perhaps we might consider a hypothetical situation: Suppose a traffic accident occurs at an intersection, and there are two witnesses to it. One is a pedestrian waiting to cross the street, and the other is in the car following one of the vehicles involved. Which of the witnesses will an investigator want to hear from to determine what actually happened?

The answer, of course, is that the investigator will interview both witnesses in order to get the best impression of what happened and who was responsible. The pedestrian will have seen the impact from a vantage point that was close and unobstructed by another vehicle, and the other driver will have seen it less directly, but will have been able to observe the driving pattern of at least one of the other vehicles prior to the accident: Was it speeding or moving erratically, perhaps with a distracted driver?

The point is, the investigator will need the testimony of both witnesses to get a clearer view of the accident and a deeper understanding of what happened.

This analogy helps us see the value of what we might call the "multiple witness feature" of the biblical testimony. Much of the narrative that comprises that testimony reflects the presence of often two, and sometimes more, witnesses to a given event or theme. The creation stories and the other examples noted above all provide a "dual witness" account of what they portray. In the New Testament, the gospel portraits of Jesus all reflect differences of both substance and nuance in their portrayal of him, providing a more comprehensive view of him than any one of them would provide alone.

Felix's question has opened the door to an understanding of the Bible as "testimony" comprised of different witnesses who help point beyond the details of any one version of the story to the 'truth" (often a theological affirmation) they all in their various ways are pointing to.

What is a faithful way to respond to other faiths?

A family has moved in nearby, and Arnold has done the "good neighbor thing" by reaching out to them with the kind of welcome his family experienced when they moved in a few years back. The new neighbors have responded graciously, and the families have become good friends.

It became clear early on that the new neighbors are Muslim in their faith and practice. They are active in the local mosque, and the mother and daughters reflect some of the traditional patterns of dress. This has not been an obstacle of any kind for their participation in the neighborhood, as might be feared in some settings. They join in happily and generously in neighborhood activities—cookouts, yard sales, and care and maintenance of common areas.

Arnold grew up in a traditional evangelical church family, which emphasized the importance of hospitality, love and respect for one's neighbor; and he has enjoyed getting to know in a personal way some things about the faith of Islam beyond what he had simply heard about. He is impressed with his neighbors' devotion, and he notes the compassion and generosity with which they relate to their new neighbors.

Arnold's own background planted deeply in his experience the belief that the Christian faith is the only "true" faith, and that Christians have an obligation to witness to that truth, and to seek to bring others to it. He remembers Jesus' saying "I am the way, the truth and the life; no one comes to the Father but by me" being emphasized a lot, reinforced by captivating stories of missionaries who came back from the far corners of the world, having courageously followed their evangelical calling.

There is a bit of understandable tension in Arnold's mind as he tries to relate this deep-seated influence of his own beliefs to his growing friendship with his neighbors of another faith.

This is not the first time the question has come up for him about the relation of his faith to that of others in his life. In high school he had a number of friends who were Jewish, and he became familiar with some of the elements of their tradition, even participating with them on occasion in some of the festivals and observances. It did not occur to any of them to let their religious differences interfere with the friendship they enjoyed.

Still, he remembers that occasionally the teaching of his own faith, as he had experienced it, left him with a nagging question about how he should relate to those who did not share it. Was he compromising his faith by not trying to persuade them to see the truth as he had experienced it?

That question dissipated as they graduated and moved on with their lives in different directions. But now he finds it coming back at a different stage of his life in his relationship with his neighbors. He and his family now are active members of a church fellowship that is warm and inclusive, quite diverse in religious background, race, and social status, but still one that assumes that faith in Christ is the only way to salvation and a "right" relationship with God. This is not pushed in an aggressive or crusading way, as has been the case in some Christian settings, but the assumption is not questioned in any overt way.

So, Arnold finds himself with a mostly private faith challenge: he has believed for a long time the teaching of his church that "the Christian way is the only way," and now he is experiencing first hand the devotion and lifestyle of a family, much like his own, whose faith expresses itself in an admirable, yet different way.

His first step in "taking his question public" was to ask his minister over coffee one day how he dealt with the question, confident that it would have accompanied him in his work in the community. The minister listened attentively and affirmed Arnold's practice of Christian hospitality in his relationships with his neighbors of another faith. He also indicated that he has come to be concerned about the exclusive implications of a "Jesus only" theology in a community of other faiths.

They both acknowledged the deeply rooted place of this belief in their church, and its influence on the generations of evangelical and missionary ministry who have worked to spread the gospel and "win the world for Christ." They both also affirmed the powerful transforming effect of what God has disclosed to them in and through the life and teachings of Jesus Christ. Being Christian is in essence who they are spiritually, and they cannot help seeing life and faith through this lens.

Still, their experience with friends and neighbors who see life and faith from another vantage point has raised understandable questions about the assumed claim that theirs is the only way to see. Some will probably encourage them to "double down" on their traditional belief that the Christian way is the only way, while others may counsel them to "relativize" the matter in a direction of: "It doesn't matter what you believe as long as you're sincere."

Which of the keys might help unlock the dilemma that Arnold and his minister are facing? If we were invited into their conversation, how would we respond?

Perhaps a good start for us in responding to the question would be to think about whether and when this question has been ours. When and where did an emphasis of "Jesus is the only way" become a part of our experience? When and where did encounters and experience raise questions about that belief, and how did we respond to them? What thoughts and ideas were helpful in thinking through the question?

Our Key #10 contains some observations about how responses to this question have accompanied the Christian faith family throughout its history and especially in an age of increasing religious pluralism. "Can I be right if you're not wrong?" is often the first form the question takes, as a deep commitment to one's own "truth" is a natural consequence of what we have described as a faith experience.

Both Arnold and his minister acknowledge the tension built into the question between a commitment to what one has experienced as true and a respect and openness to the truth of others' experience that is different. They seem to have a readiness to embrace a way to move beyond the tension and to hold to the two values (commitment and openness) without having to sacrifice one for the sake of the other. Is there a way to understand their Christian faith that opens a door for the kind of community they wish to have, both theologically and socially, with people of other faiths?

Perhaps some conversation on the natural process of movement from exclusive thinking in an inclusive direction in other areas of life could be helpful. As experience broadens from first encounters and impressions, there is a natural widening of perspective of acceptance of things that are new and previously unfamiliar. In most growth and personal development, there is a gradual evolution from "me thinking" to "we thinking," which opens the possibility and provides the basis for community.

Beyond that for our present question, there is the sticky issue of what we have been taught about the exclusiveness of the Christian faith, and, more specifically, some direct affirmations in the Bible that support exclusiveness.

 Since one of those affirmations often becomes part of conversations on this topic, perhaps it will be helpful to take a more detailed look at it here as part of "polishing the key" and opening the possibility for its use.

The particular text, you will not be surprised by now to see, is that statement in John 14:6 where Jesus is reported to say, "I am the way, the truth, and the life. No one comes to the Father except by/through me."

If we were looking for explicit biblical support for an exclusivist perspective, we would not likely find a clearer example. Because of its direct relevance to our question, it deserves some careful analysis. Two features of the text offer deeper insights. One has to do with the context, the other with the content of the saying.

The saying is part of some verses intended to be words of comfort: "Do not let your hearts be troubled. Believe in God. Believe in me. In my Father's house are many dwelling places... there is place for you ... and you know the way to the place where I am going." Then Thomas, whose faith seeking understanding plays a prominent role in the theology of the Fourth Gospel, says, "Lord, we do not know where you are going. How can we know the way?"

This is the immediate context of the statement in 14:6—it is to Thomas's question that the exclusivist-sounding "I am the way" statement is made.

If we look carefully at the statement itself, we can observe a feature of it that is not as exclusivist as it appears on the surface, and it might open the possibility of a more inclusive understanding. Here I ask you to be patient with something a little more technical.

In the Greek language of the New Testament, the use of personal pronouns as the subject of a sentence is usually not necessary because of the way that verbs are conjugated to indicate whether the subject is first person, second person, or third person (also singular or plural). For example, a statement such as "He went to the store" would need only to say, "Went to the store," since the form off the verb would indicate third person singular—no need for the pronoun.

In this kind of syntax, if the pronoun *is* used, it is for the purpose of adding emphasis, in the way that we would italicize, underline, use all caps, or "bold" our word: **HE** went to the store.

In the text, "I am the way, the truth and the life ...," the personal pronoun is used, which suggests that the line is intended to be read, "*I* am the way ...."

It is perfectly natural to read the line in English and place the emphasis where it seems most obvious: on the word "the"—"I am **the** way, **the** truth, and **the** life." But the Greek text suggests that in response to Thomas' question about "the way," Jesus pulls the answer back from a specific path to the whole of himself as the way: "It is *I*, Thomas—everything about me and who I am—that is the way—not only what you understand about me at this point, but everything that comes to your understanding, and everything that will remain beyond your understanding—that is the way."

The implication of this subtle technical point is that the "way" is the full reality of who Jesus is, which will always be more than any person or group can possess exclusively.

A collateral text that supports this suggestion is found in the imagery of the shepherd and the sheep that Jesus uses in John 10:7-11 and 16 to speak of his relation to humanity: "I (pronoun used) am the gate for the sheep ... I (pronoun again) am the gate... and whoever enters by me will be saved, and will come in and go out and find pasture. ... I (yes, pronoun again) am the good shepherd. I know my own and my own know me, just as the Father knows me and I know the Father. I (no pronoun) have other sheep that do not belong to this fold. I must bring them also, and they will listen to my voice. So, there will be one flock, one shepherd."

These two texts and their emphasis on the whole of who Jesus is—his way of life, his teachings, his transparency to the will of God—as the "way" is more compatible with the universal scope of the WORD becoming flesh that is the theme of John's gospel—suggesting that the "way" may be broader and more inclusive than the experience of a given group of disciples can claim as an exclusive possession. It is the inclusive "I" rather than the exclusive "the" that dominates "I am the way, the truth, and the life."

Arnold and his minister consider the possibility of seeing the "Jesus way" in the lives and commitment of the Muslim neighbors; and, in doing so, perhaps they will continue their search for deeper understanding of who Jesus is, even for themselves. This key may have unlocked a door to more faithful communion with another part of God's family.

How do we apply the Bible's evolving moral guidance?

Jeremy is a medical student who has recently joined with a local faith community as a way of maintaining a long commitment to his faith and of making wider connections with people beyond his professional training. This church was recommended to him as one that was open-minded, progressive, and welcoming to a diverse population.

He has been attending a "faith and issues" class that seeks to be a forum for questions and discoveries of how faith operates in the intersection of a biblical heritage and the challenges of modern life. In a discussion of how the Bible helps us in responding to various pressing moral issues of the day, he raises a question that has puzzled him as he has thought about this.

He observes that the Bible doesn't seem to speak with the same voice on many issues of moral concern, for example:

- Some scriptures call for a faithful response to an injury or injustice with an "eye for an eye" kind of retaliation, while others counsel us not to return in kind such abuse but to "turn the other cheek."
- Some scriptures condone slavery and give guidance on how masters and slaves are to relate to each other, whereas others affirm "In Christ there is neither Jew nor Greek, slave nor free ...."
- Some scriptures portray marriage as an inviolable partnership between one man and one woman, but elsewhere polygamy is openly practiced among God's covenant people.

In addition, Jeremy points out that the Bible speaks little or not at all to many of the moral issues of our time that involve his medical world—issues such as abortion, euthanasia, gay and transgender rights and protection, and genetic engineering. How, he asks, can we follow biblical guidance when that guidance is so unclear?

His questions are serious ones, shared by many who seek to be faithful to a heritage and at the same time responsible in the issues and decisions that are required to function in the modern world. Theology, as faith seeking understanding, has this question as part of its task; and theologians, both the formal and the everyday variety, attempt to find and affirm the connection between faith and the challenge of the issue.

We can begin by asking which key/keys in our collection is/are most relevant to what we are being asked to do.

Since the issue of moral guidance often connects the question at hand with the foundational source of faith that we have in the Bible, the key that focuses on the nature of the biblical testimony and the character of its guidance is likely to be the first one to use (Key #4).

Again, we would commend Jeremy for the discernment reflected in his question, for indeed there is some diversity in what the Bible reflects in its moral implications. Such recognition is a first step in moving theological thinking in a positive and healthy direction.

We have entered the arena of theological thinking known as ethics—the reflection and application of a faith's values to decisions made in response to the challenges of life. In short, ethics is the response to the question, "How do we decide what to do and to think in the everyday decisions that affect our own life and the lives of others?" And, in the context of Christian faith, the question most always looks to the Bible for help.

Jeremy has noticed that the Bible is not always clear in its guidance. There are differences in what is considered faithful in different parts of the testimony. How is one to know how to "be biblical" in one's thinking and deciding, when there are options that can support varying, even contradictory, viewpoints on an issue?

Jeremy observed that in places the Bible supports slavery, while in other places it offers a pattern of faithful relationships that would make the "owning" of one person by another contrary to God's agenda for the human family. A fellow "faith and issues" classmate noted that strong arguments based on the Bible for and against slavery were prominent among Christian leaders during the three decades leading up to the American Civil War. Another classmate mentioned that the founding of their own denomination was based on a defense of slavery against those who sought to abolish it.

Examples of opposing viewpoints continued to emerge in the discussion, including: the elaborate systems of penalties for offense and injury in the law codes of Leviticus vs. the teaching of Jesus on mercy, forgiveness, and non-retaliation; the place of women in the hyper-patriarchal world of the early testimony vs. the somewhat revolutionary inclusion of women that began to emerge in the early church.

This "faith and issues" class was confronting a familiar response to issues on which there is disagreement in the scriptures: "The Bible says it, I believe it, and that settles it."

Application of our Key #4 on the nature of the Bible as an evolving "testimony" of many generations of a covenant community speaks to this challenge. It helps us see various stages of an ancient culture, and it reflects the development over time of their understanding of their faith as they lived out their calling.

Seeing the Bible in this way should alleviate any surprise that in places it reflects patterns of thought and cultural features that were part of the ancient or early Christian world. And, it should encourage us to ask in what direction the testimony seems to be pointing as a realization of a covenant community based on the transforming covenant promise: "I will be with you and will make you a blessing to all people."

Jeremy's question and the discussion that followed it led his class to a consideration of how the covenant ethics of the Bible evolved from its earliest expressions toward what it would become in the later parts of the covenant journey.

The group discovered that the earliest expressions of the testimony reflected a "straight obedience" ethics: Do what God says, get the rewards for doing so, and experience the penalty of disobedience. Rules and regulations soon appear in detail, indicating obedient living and the consequences of not following them. The emerging rigidity of these rules and the ease of getting around them for personal gain and power led the prophets to call out the hypocrisy of seeming to be faithful while engaging in all manner of injustice and idolatry. By the time of Jesus, those rules still had the kind of authority that fueled the religious leaders' objections to Jesus' tendency to put personal needs ahead of "keeping the Law." The needs of people and of the community's well-being were taking priority over the more legalistic adherence to a rule-based ethics.

In Paul's writing, the study group found two things in particular that helped illustrate this evolution. One was his response to the Galatians who were challenged by an insistence on the part of some Jewish-background Christians that Gentiles who joined as followers of Christ be subjected to the initiation rites of Judaism first—rules are rules, they believed. Paul responded that these rules of the Law did not apply to those whose lives had been transformed by their experience with Christ. In terms of our consideration, an embrace of covenant faith and its transformation superseded the rules (at least some of them) that had accompanied and guided its earlier manifestation.

The second feature of Paul's ethical guidance the group found in 1 Corinthians 8, where Paul responds to a question about the eating of meat that had been originally offered as an act of worship to an idol. One is free from the rule that prohibits that, he said, but one must "take care, lest one's exercise of that freedom become a 'stumbling block' to others," who may not have arrived at that stage of faith-freedom. Here the class found an ethics of love and concern for the well-being of others to be the primary ethical guidance in the exercise of one's freedom.

They discovered that the moral guidance of the biblical testimony reflects an evolution from a "follow the rules" ethics in its early stages to a more holistic ethics that placed decisions and actions in the larger framework of human community—an ethics of broad-based love over the narrower focus of rules.

Jeremy's question led the everyday theologians to do some good work in discovering that the moral guidance of the biblical testimony is more a trajectory pointing to what is the essence of faithful living than a code by which one can check off personal righteousness.

How do we bridge the gap between faith and science?

Frances and Doris are grandmothers and retired elementary school teachers who have worked for many years in the children's area of their church's education program.

They also participate in some adult study groups that explore biblical literature with the help of ongoing biblical scholarship, and they have become aware of the origins and nature of the biblical testimony. After being a bit challenging at first, it has been liberating to learn that the Bible was composed over many generations by people whose understanding of the world was very different from that of modern readers.

With their long experience of working with children, Frances and Doris have become quite creative and effective in helping children enjoy and remember the general Bible stories that carry the Bible's testimony forward. They introduce creation, the stories of Abraham, Jacob and his sons, Moses, Joshua, Samuel, David, the prophets, and of course the stories about Jesus and Paul.

The material these teachers use does a good job of presenting the Bible stories in a colorful way, so that the children have a clear picture of the Garden of Eden with Adam and Eve and the serpent and what God means for them to be and do there. They have a vivid understanding of Moses leading the children of Israel across the sea with walls of water on each side. They are fascinated by God stopping the sun in the sky to allow Joshua more time to finish off a battle.

Because these stories are presented to the children as though they happened and were recorded the same way that last week's news is reported, Frances and Doris have begun to wonder what will happen as the children's experiences expand to encounter different understandings of how the world came to be and how parts of the story are crafted to communicate religious faith and concepts more than historical facts.

Is there a way to teach these stories and the truths they embody, while at the same time helping the children understand them as the way an ancient people saw life in a world that they understood differently from the way we understand ours?

The question has to do with both our Key #4 on the nature of the Bible as a primary source for theological understanding, and Key #8 on the relation of faith and science. Frances and Doris have no problem themselves with the distinction between scientific thinking and religious thinking, and they understand our principle that every religious affirmation of faith is accompanied by the scientific understanding of the natural world that is contemporary with it.

Their question is when and how to introduce that kind of discernment into children's experience, so that they won't find themselves later in a place where they feel they must choose between "believing the Bible" and believing what science has enabled them to learn about our world.

It is here, I believe, that everyday theologians such as our hypothetical teachers can make a significant contribution to the "faith (of children) seeking understanding." Many an intellectual and theological crisis can be avoided if a framework is suggested early in a person's development that promotes a partnership rather than a rivalry between what a faith experience is led to claim and what the results of generations of scientific and historical investigation and discovery have made available to our understanding of the world in which we live.

Perhaps the most natural way to contribute to the maturing faith of children is to relate the Bible stories to other kinds of stories that children learn with different levels of truth and meaning to them, suggesting that these are special stories designed to help us think about God and God's relation to the world. And sometimes, long ago, people understood the world in ways that are different from how we understand it.

Teachers can build in the subliminal message: "When you grow up, you may help us discover new things and new ways of thinking that we can't imagine now. Who would have ever thought just a few years ago that we would have cell phones and send people to outer space and to the moon? Science is always changing the ways we understand our world, and God is with us all the time, helping us to discover and learn from those changes."

Frances and Doris fully understand and appreciate the importance of helping children engage and remember the stories that provide the foundation and framework for their particular faith tradition, but they also hope to plant the seeds for them to understand the nature and depth of those stories so that they will minimize what they have to "unlearn" as they mature in their faith journey.

How does faith respond when bad things happen?

One of the experiences in life where faith and its theology—formal and everyday—are put to a crucial test is in responding to events and circumstances where loss and suffering find their way into our lives. Accidents, illnesses, destructive crimes, natural and ill-motivated catastrophes, and private expressions of cruelty and abuse touch our lives in too many ways to ignore.

In such times and circumstances, faith's first question seems naturally to be "Why?" The answer, however it comes, is an expression of that faith's understanding of what faith means in this most extreme of experiences. In other words, the response is nothing more and nothing less than faith seeking understanding—an expression of theology.

Formal theologians—the clerics and the academics—have struggled with this question for centuries, and the challenge carries the general label of "the problem of evil." The responses to that struggle have come collectively to be called "theodicy" (from *theos* and *dikaios*, meaning affirming God's justice or righteousness). The literature that has come out of that struggle is massive and worthy of study and continued refinement, but for our purposes I will focus on the personal theological challenge of how to respond faithfully to our fellow pilgrims when the problem of evil strikes home.

Certainly, there are better and worse ways to respond to faith's question. Our responses will be clear expressions of the theology that is at work seeking its own understanding. Explicitly, but more often implicitly, what we say and do in response will communicate our understanding of God, our understanding of God's relation to the world and human experience, and our understanding of the nature of the covenant relationship we have called faith.

The simple expression of the problem of evil goes like this: If God is all powerful and perfectly good, then God could and would keep bad things from happening. But bad things happen. Therefore, God must be either not all powerful or not perfectly good.

Notice that this "problem" is not in the bad things that happen, as horrible as they often are, but in how we think about God in relation to the bad things that happen—the "problem" is theological.

So, from here the range of responses to the "why?" question cover a number of possibilities that seek to "justify" God's power and goodness in the face of such obvious challenges. Consider the following:

- God lets bad things happen as a punishment for disobedience, bad decisions, and general sinfulness.
- God lets bad things happen to serve as a test for people's faithfulness.
- God lets bad things happen to teach lessons about priorities and responsibility.
- God has no relationship to the things that happen—they just happen.

- God has a plan into which all things—good and bad—fit that we cannot understand.
- God uses bad things to make us stronger.
- God needed another angel in heaven (in response to the death of a child).
- Rest assured that this (bad thing) is a part of God's will.
- This is awful—it's OK to be mad at God. God can take it.
- "We'll understand it all better by and by."

These are a few of the responses that well-meaning persons sometimes offer in an attempt to help another with the suffering of being victim to the variety of bad things." Notice that, probably without meaning to do so, the responses tend to seem more concerned with justifying a particular belief about God than they do with offering comfort and support to the victim of the pain and suffering.

The responses are theology in the sense that they are faith seeking understanding in the face of terrible tragedy/loss. The question that comes from our first conceptual key on the relation of faith and theology is this: Does the response reflect the covenant relationship that faith is, or is it more an effort to affirm and adhere to certain of the beliefs that accompany that relationship? To put it another way: Is my response to this person an effort to be an agent of the transforming mystery of a faith relationship, or is it an effort to defend some particular way of thinking about that relationship and its God?

I have not suggested a hypothetical example to illustrate the application of the keys to this particular challenge for everyday theologians, because we *are* the examples, and the issue is not hypothetical. How does our refinement and use of the "keys" help us to do the work of theology that is called for as we respond to this part of our life in the community of faith and beyond?

We have noted just now how Key #1 reminds us not to let our theology that seeks to understand our faith become a substitute for the relationship that faith is. And, Key #2 reminds us not to let the beliefs that accompany our faith at a given time shift from being a description and pointer to our faith to being a definition of it.

Key #4 invites us to embrace and use the Bible as a source in faith's quest for understanding, so it will be appropriate to ask what kind of guidance we can find there for this arena of theological work. Let's take a look at how it handles this question.

Our first reminder is that the Bible is an evolving testimony of a people's journey as a covenant community. It reflects a variety of theological understandings of what that covenant faith means, as we can see a trajectory from its earliest expressions to its more mature ones that invites us to see a process we can join.

Within this testimony, we can see that the Bible engages in a "conversation with itself" on many elements of the covenant faith. We often see the "dual witness" phenomenon we noted earlier, where two (and sometimes more than two) sides of a story's meaning are offered side by side in the testimony.

On our current question of a theological understanding of the relation of God to the bad things that happen, we can see that internal conversation in a number of ways. There are indications that disobedience and faithlessness are met with punishment. Adam's and Eve's expulsion from the garden (Genesis 3), Moses' punishment for striking the rock with his stick to get water (Num. 20:1-3), Uzzah's being struck dead for touching the Ark of the Covenant (2 Sam. 6:6-7), the death of Bathsheba's first born as punishment for David's egregious sin of adultery and murder (2 Sam. 12:14), and the prophets' assessment of the loss of Temple and city to Babylon as a consequence of Judah's centuries of corruption and injustice: these are among many examples of this theological response to why these things happened.

But the biblical testimony takes us beyond this punishment perspective in its continuing conversation with itself. The classic and unparalleled treatment of the issue of why bad things happen is found in the Old Testament book of Job. The familiar story of the righteous and faithful man who falls victim to all manner of misfortune in a dramatic challenge and demonstration of faithfulness illustrates both the inadequacy of this punitive theology and the mystery of faith's profound trust in the face of tragedy.

When Job's hardships—admittedly presented in the story as a test of his faith—befall him, his friends come to his side and sit with him for days. Eventually they begin to offer their theological responses to his suffering. Their argument generally goes like this: "It is obvious that you have committed some sort of sin, or this would not have befallen you. Why don't you confess your sin, repent, and then the Lord will surely redeem you?"

Job protests that he is innocent and therefore will not commit the sin of dishonesty in order to escape his situation—his faith means more to him than that.

After a lengthy exchange, Job takes his case directly to the Lord, declaring his efforts to be and do the right thing in all ways, while at the same time expressing his perplexity at what has happened to him. He is essentially protesting what is to him the injustice of his situation, and he calls the Lord to account for that.

The Lord responds with a reframing of Job's question in the larger framework of the mystery of a covenant faith, where the Creator partner's participation embraces the universal, while the creature partner's participation is limited to the particular. The theology of this profound story points to our Key #3 on the partiality of our understanding at any given time in our lifelong quest of faith seeking understanding.

The "take-away" from this part of the Bible's guidance for our theological work in responding to circumstances of suffering and loss is that our efforts to offer answers to the "why?" question of suffering do not express the deeper truth that lies in the mystery of a trusting covenant faith.

The New Testament offers two particular insights that relate directly to this theological challenge. One is the account in the Fourth Gospel where Jesus and the disciples come upon a man who has been blind all his life (John 9). The disciples, reflecting a theology that understands misfortune and handicaps as a consequence of sin, ask, "Master, who sinned, this man or his parents, that he was born blind?"

They are essentially asking the causal "why?" question: What caused this man's blindness? He couldn't have sinned before he was born, and it wouldn't seem quite right for him to be punished for his parents' sin of some sort. We can imagine that they might have been proud of themselves for coming up with a good question for their teacher.

Jesus doesn't answer their question, but tells them they are actually asking the wrong one. The question is not what caused the man's blindness (the "why" of cause), but how is it an occasion for the healing power of God to be shown (the "why" of purpose).

Notice how Jesus' response (and the healing act that follows) redirects the natural and understandable question of cause to the more theologically focused question of how faith works in response. It is a shift from a "why?" to a "what now?"

However we understand the nature of the healing miracles that are a significant part of the gospel narratives, this account underscores a point consistent with the Job story: The "answer" to the problem of evil lies not in a level of understanding that claims to know "why" something has happened, but in the trust that is rooted in the mystery of a covenant relationship whose core promise is "I will be with you."

The second point from the New Testament that offers some guidance for out thinking on this issue is a small but interesting technical point that has important theological implications. It is a familiar verse from Paul's letter to the Romans (8:28).

The translation of that verse, based on the most numerous of the available ancient manuscripts of Paul's letters, reads this way: "We know that all things work together for good for those who love God and are called according to his purpose." An alternative translation, interestingly based on the oldest extant manuscript of Romans, reads slightly differently: "We know that God works all things together for good for those who love God and are called according to his purpose."

Notice that in the more familiar translation the subject of the verb "work together" is "all things," implying that faith affirms things will eventually work out by moving toward good results. The less familiar, but most likely closest to the original, wording has "God" as the subject of the verb "work together," implying that it is not the "things" that work together for good, but that God works together in all things toward the good. The subtle but significant theological implication is that faith sees God as "working together" (note the relational/covenantal connotation of the verb) in all things according to a purpose that lies beyond them. There is no effort here to make the "all things" good, but an affirmation that, whatever the "things" are, the covenant promise—"I will be with you"—is operative.

This is perhaps too tedious a tour of the Bible's attention to this difficult part of the covenant journey, but I hope it underscores the point that our inevitable responses to the problem of suffering and loss reflect a theological perspective that can either serve our need to be able to answer the "why" question, or they can serve our fellow pilgrims' need to experience a presence that affirms they are not alone. Here the work of theology is not to provide an answer, but to put another shoulder under the load of the question. "I am with you."

Rabbi Harold Kushner, whose popular book, *When Bad Things Happen to Good People*, helped a generation of readers with the relation of faith to the tragic and otherwise unfortunate experiences of life, tells the story of a little boy who was late coming home. When his mother asked why he was late, he replied that he had come upon a boy who was crying because his bicycle was broken and he stopped to help him. His mother asked how he could help him—he didn't know anything about fixing a bicycle. He replied, "I stopped and helped him cry."

…Theology as shared tears—something "everyday theologians" do all the time—the shared presence that reaches across the boundary of words and their limitations.

Part 3

Supplemental Keys on Particular Topics

Keys to Certain Doors of the Theological House

As we can see from our hypothetical examples of the kinds of conversations that everyday theologians can find themselves in, the questions that emerge from the faith journey can be complex and challenging. I hope the basic conceptual keys provide some distinctions and frameworks for responding in helpful ways to those who share the journey.

As noted in the introduction, most of the conceptual keys have grown out of the long privilege I have enjoyed working with students in the context of academic religious studies. Their questions, observations, and willingness to think with me about matters of faith have been distilled into the ten general keys we have considered. Former students who may read this result of our shared pilgrimage may well see their own contributions to the suggestions that are set forth, even though they are framed as hypothetical applications. If and when they do, I hope they will be aware of my deep appreciation for the gift of their insights.

In this concluding section, I would like to add some additional concepts and ways of thinking that pertain to a few particular topics that seem to emerge as a concern when features of the faith of our Christian tradition are studied in depth.

While they are not "keys" in the sense of the ones that help unlock general areas of theological thinking, they are patterns of thought that develop once the rooms of the theological house are unlocked and entered to continue the process of faith seeking understanding.

I include them here as supplemental keys to continue the image, but they are essentially observations and reflections of things I have noticed as the process of theological thinking moves along on the pilgrimage—refinements and sometimes redirections of faith's understanding as traditional formulas and beliefs receive the benefit of careful study.

They are arranged here in no particular order, just as the questions and challenges that come to everyday theologians don't come in any particular order. I invite you to reflect on your own experience with the particular topics and to add your own thoughts to a consideration of how we might participate in others' thinking about these issues.

The "Inspiration" of the Bible

It seems to be typical at the beginning of the faith journey in our tradition to hear the affirmation that the Bible is "the inspired Word of God." This affirmation clearly intends to point to the Bible's special uniqueness as a source of guidance and a lifelong companion in the faith journey. The Bible is typically the first place of appeal when faith questions arise, and it has served through the centuries as comfort, moral guide, confrontation, challenge, and assurance of hope for the generations of the covenant family.

The nature of "divine inspiration" (literally the "God-breathing") of scripture has received a wide range of interpretation, and there is a noticeable progression of understanding in that interpretation in the experience of many who embrace the Bible's authority as a foundational guide for faith's understanding. That range of interpretation extends from what is sometimes referred to as the "plenary verbal" understanding of inspiration, which holds that the original wording of the biblical text originated with God and was passed to the original writers who recorded it faithfully and with perfect accuracy. One can imagine a kind of stenographic dictation depicted in artistic renderings showing a biblical writer with an image of divine guidance over his shoulder telling him what to write.

Other interpretations suggest a less direct form of inspiration, in which ideas are revealed and individual authors use their own words to communicate them. This interpretation accounts for variations of both writing style and variations in understanding of the natural world and of history.

When questions arise about the places where the Bible seems to have contradictions, there is concern about how this could happen in a book whose truth is divinely inspired. Advocates of this understanding of inspiration often point to the long process of preservation and translation as the reason for the discrepancies, affirming that the original texts (no longer available) were inerrant and that our current versions bear the marks of changes over time, all the while maintaining that the essential message of the Bible is unaffected by these flaws.

When the Bible is studied carefully over time, especially with regard to its textual complexity, the historical context of its formulation, and the scope and trajectory of its theological purpose, there tends to be a shift in students' minds about its being an inspired text, at least in the sense affirmed by the versions of a dictation theory of inspiration.

As we noted in Key #4, a careful and thorough study of the nature and development of the Bible points to seeing it as a collective testimony of many generations of the covenant journey. In it we see many voices speaking from the intersections of their covenant calling giving expression to the meaning of their faith.

Thinking of the Bible as a testimony, rather than some version of "Holy Writ" (in the sense of a mechanically delivered text from God), tends to shift from a concept of an inspired text to a text produced by an inspired people—still inspired, profoundly so in the ebbs and flows of human experience, but less mechanical and dictational, and more an expression of the faith it invites its readers to embrace.

So, I offer this supplemental key: the difference between an inspired text and a text produced by an inspired people. Which kind of inspiration does the Bible reflect in your reading and embrace of it? This key for understanding the inspiration of the Bible can unlock the opportunity not only for believing what it says, but also for seeing what it sees and for becoming a part of the biblical story which continues to be written in every generation.

The Old Testament Prophets

Another transitional concept that occurs for students who engage the literature of the Old Testament involves the portrayal of the prophetic element of the covenant faith. In popular usage and in first impressions that many readers have of the Hebrew prophets, the tendency is to think of them as fortune tellers—persons with special gifts for predicting what will happen in the future. Indeed, the early prophets do seem to reflect these special powers, often accompanied by ecstatic dancing and chanting (1 Sam. 10:1-13). Samuel himself, often described as the pioneer of the biblical prophets, is cast as a "seer" who can locate lost animals and offer other divine guidance (1 Sam. 9:19-20).

Soon, though, we begin to see an evolution in the concept of prophecy that moves in the direction of an ethical consciousness and a passion for justice. Nathan confronts King David with his heinous act of adultery and murder in its cover-up (2 Sam. 12:1-15). Elijah confronts King Ahab for his murder of Naboth and the theft of his vineyard (1 Kgs. 21:1-29). Micaiah ben Imlah carries this "speaking truth to power" to the limit as he goes against the 400 court prophets to tell the king the truth about a planned military campaign (1 Kgs. 22:1-53).

The "writing prophets" of the eight century BCE—whose books we have by their names, Amos, Hosea, Isaiah of Jerusalem and Micah—are the first of the category of "classical prophets," and the ones who formalize this ethical consciousness. Their focus is to speak on behalf of the covenant faith against the corruption and superficiality that has emerged in Israel from the alliance of established religion and political power.

There is a sense in which these prophets tell the future, but it is a different kind of foretelling that is often associated with those who are said to have some kind of magical ability. Their future telling is similar to that of a person who sees a pattern of bad and irresponsible decisions on the part of a friend or loved one and points to the consequences of those decisions. Not, "On April 22 next year something bad is going to happen to you." But, "If you continue this pattern, I can tell you there will be some bad results."

For the prophets of Israel and Judah, their prophecy was not based in some magical divine power, but in a deep rootage in the terms of the covenant faith and a keen insight into the ways it was being distorted in their time. The future they foretold was the looming downfall of the kingdom and the exile in Babylon—a prophecy that was clearly fulfilled.

Their future-telling was based on a deep understanding of reality informed by a knowledge of the past, keen insight into the circumstances of the present, and a clear vision of what the consequences would be. Wisdom and courage, not magic, was the basis of their prophecy.

Interestingly, when that downfall came and land, city, and temple were lost, the prophets' words of stern judgment changed in the direction of hope and restoration. While not denying the downfall and the reasons for its happening, the prophets offered a strong reminder from the covenant promise that this disaster was not the end of the faith community's story.

For example, Jeremiah's strong judgmental word about the corruption and idolatry of Judah's politico-religious alliance becomes a reminder of the hopeful promise of the new "covenant written on the heart" (Jer. 33:33). Second Isaiah's "servant poems" provide not only a hopeful assurance of restoration, but also a profound image of redemptive suffering that becomes a lens through which the early Christian community understood the nature and mission of Jesus (Isa. 42:1-4, 49:1-6, 50:1-11, 52:13–53:12).

So, this supplemental key is an observation that the concept of prophecy evolves in the Old Testament toward a "forthtelling" (rather than a "foretelling") of the covenant promise and the agenda of the covenant's God. When Jesus is referred to as the "fulfillment of prophecy," perhaps it is less that he is an event they predicted as something God was going to do, but that he is the incarnation of the voice that bears witness to what God has been doing all along.

And, this key for understanding prophecy can unlock the prophetic voice of the community of faith in all generations. There is a prophetic voice inside every everyday theologian, and there are circumstances aplenty calling for its expression.

The Gospel "Portraits" of Jesus

It is natural for those who have responded to the invitation to follow Jesus to seek to know as much as possible about him. The church and the many parts of its extended family offer an abundance of ways of thinking and believing about Jesus, so the new pilgrim is not without guidance in developing a concept of who he was—his life, his deeds, his teaching, and his place as a pivotal part of God's reconciling work.

The primary source of our understanding of Jesus is found in the New Testament gospels, and there is a key for reading and studying them that can be helpful in opening up the depths of what they have to offer.

At a first reading, the Gospels offer a report of Jesus' life, especially the part known as his public ministry—the period between his baptism and the events surrounding his crucifixion and resurrection. We read about his encounters with followers and adversaries. We see accounts of his teachings, both in parables and in longer sermon-like addresses. We follow his journey from Nazareth to Jerusalem, and we see in graphic detail the story of the last week of his life leading up to his trial and execution.

There is a tendency to read these narratives as we would a biography or a news report of a schedule of events. On closer reading, however, we might be perplexed at some of the variations in the accounts, and the different emphases that the individual gospels seem to highlight in their portrayal of him and his work.

For example, in Mark's gospel, Jesus is a "man of action," moving with some urgency from place to place, doing works of healing and restoration, encountering various kinds of resistance along the way. In Matthew, Jesus is portrayed as the fulfillment of the covenant hopes of the Hebrew scriptures—a kind of "new Moses," fulfilling and reinterpreting the Law, and functioning like the teaching rabbis of the time. Luke portrays Jesus as the special advocate for the poor and marginalized in his society, crossing traditional religious boundaries and embracing Samaritans, lepers, and those otherwise considered unacceptable. John offers still another framework for his portrayal of Jesus and offers a quite different collection of memories of his work and teaching.

How does the Bible student resolve these differences in a quest for understanding Jesus? Part of the answer, of course, lies in our earlier emphasis on seeing the biblical narratives as a testimony of witnesses to an experience of covenant faith-making. As we have seen, different witnesses to an event or experience will testify according to their particular vantage points and according to how the event or experience has impacted them. The testimony is always a mixture of the event itself and of the perspective and interpretation of the witnesses.

Beyond this, a helpful image for students of the Gospels has been to consider them as "portraits" rather than "photographs" of Jesus. Consider the distinction: A photograph of a subject is an exact reproduction of an image that passes through a camera lens and is recorded digitally or on film. There is little room for interpretation or nuance—what the camera sees is what you get. A portrait, painted by an artist, is a different kind of thing. An artist might well spend some time getting to know the subject, if not already known, and he or she will be able to incorporate impressions of the subject's character and personality (gentleness, determination, etc.), perhaps emphasizing certain physical features that are distinguishing. The picture is certainly the likeness of the subject, but it may be somewhat different from a similar portrait created by another artist, and it would most likely be different from a photograph of the subject.

Thinking of the New Testament gospels as portraits of Jesus leads us to consider their origin and development and the effect of that process on what we have before us as we read and study them. The creators of the Gospels drew from the collective memory of the early Christian community those events and experiences that were memorable and transformative for them. And the narratives they provided would have been intended to respond to the life and needs of the community at the time of their writing.

Mark, for example, is believed to have been written during the time of Roman persecution under the notorious Emperor Nero, about 40 years after Jesus' life; and Jesus is portrayed as a man of action, dealing with various levels of conflict. Matthew is believed to have followed much of Mark's gospel a generation later, when concerns over the relation of the Christian movement to the covenant faith of Israel were in the forefront, and in this gospel Jesus is the fulfillment of the Law and the Prophets, and a teaching rabbi par excellence. Luke, relatively contemporary with Matthew, portrays Jesus responding to the issue of the relation of the covenant faith and the inclusion of Gentiles by portraying him as the champion and advocate of the poor and marginalized, and other outsiders. The Fourth Gospel adopts a different framework and presents Jesus as the incarnation of the *Logos*, the universal principle of reality in Greek thought, lifting his significance to an intimate relation and equality with God. This emphasis helps to make the case for the universalizing of the gospel.

This brief description of the distinctive character of each of the gospel portraits helps us to see the mixture of the subject (Jesus) and the artists (the early Christian community) in the portrayals we have. If we had video recordings of Jesus' life and work, they would be exclusively the subject, without any of the experience, perception, and understanding of his followers. The fact that we have in them their collective memory, refined over time by its application to the challenges of living their calling in a world that was both receptive and hostile to their testimony of their experience, gives us a portrait that is less precise and factually accurate than a photograph would be, but more indicative of the transformative faith that emerged from the artists' encounter with this personal disclosure of the nature and character of God.

Everyday theologians ask two questions of the Gospels: (1) What can we learn about Jesus here? (2) What can we learn here about the community that came to be from their encounter with him and who continued to live out that encounter in their world? Both subject and artist are present in these portraits.

The Bible as Source and Companion for the Faith Journey

It has been interesting to watch how the biblical testimony functions in the life of those who are on the Christian pilgrimage. It is one of the first things associated with faith, often given to children as they are beginning to read, in the hope that it will be thought of as an important part of their religious experience. Education within the faith family will feature a growing awareness of the significance of its teachings about life.

There seems to be a pattern to a maturing relationship with the Bible among those who continue to study it, and understanding this process/pattern offers a key insight into the trajectory of its function.

In early experience, the Bible is a collection of stories and teachings that invite attention to an ancient people whose experience demonstrates what being a faith community can be. It is a kind of picture that plants in readers' minds images and ideas that become a framework for thinking about how to live.

At some point in that journey, insights begin to emerge that connect those stories and events with life as it is lived in real time. The story of Joseph and his brothers might well lead to a "Hey, that's like how we want to treat each other sometimes." A parable of Jesus might lead to a comparison to an encounter at school. The picture then becomes a mirror to see something of ourselves in the story or experience—a new level of function.

Over time, another function can emerge that changes the relationship with the Bible again. The picture that became a mirror in which to see ourselves becomes a lens through which to see everything else. The process of learning what the Bible says and of incorporating the meaning of what it reveals about human experience is an important and necessary pattern of engagement with it. Building on that leads to a place of seeing what the Bible sees—looking at the world and everything in it through the lens of the testimony's reflection of the vision that guides the covenant journey.

Everyday theologians are in a place to facilitate this process by asking the questions and offering the suggestions that help fellow faith-seekers of understanding to move toward seeing their world through a biblical lens. This suggests that being a biblical people means moving along in a process from believing what the Bible says to seeing what the Bible sees.

Traditional Concepts That "Grow Up" Theologically

As a final key for the work of everyday theologians, I would like to offer an observation that has emerged from my own experience and from observing the experience of others. It has to do with what happens to some traditional concepts that are part of thinking and interpreting the faith experience. They are specific, though not limited, to the content of Christian faith and reflection; and it is hard to imagine theological thought and communication without their presence.

I am thinking of the concepts of God, Jesus, the Holy Spirit, humanity, the church, sin and salvation, the nature and destiny of history, and countless other concepts that live in various parts of the faith family. As we have noted earlier, many of these concepts are formalized into doctrines that become more or less authoritative in the "official" understandings of the realities to which they point. Once they arrive at this stage of development, they remain as guidelines for the community's thinking about their respective topics, with at least a measure of flexibility to allow for refinement and change, as the human journey and continued reflection make adjustments to new challenges.

The suggestion here is that in the life of everyday theologians, these concepts have a developmental pattern to them as well. The fact that our concepts of things and experiences grow and change with time and experience is obvious when we think about other areas of life. For example, one's concept of education has a particular form and scope when one is in elementary school, and that concept grows and matures over the course of years to be quite different and more complex by the time one is in college. A concept of patriotism and citizenship may be quite simply a respect for certain symbols at an early age, which will certainly mature to a deeper and more complex commitment and responsibility in adulthood.

For the religious dimension of our lives, and our theological reflection on it, the concepts that are the currency of that reflection seem to undergo a similar pattern of growth and refinement as the relationship of faith matures.

Is there a pattern to the maturation process of one's concept of God, of Jesus, of the church, of sin, of salvation as the journey of faith processes these concepts in the matrix of faith's challenges and responses? I believe there is.

An earlier key (#3) invited us to think about the difference between a given reality and our concept of that reality, and that distinction is relevant here. Our concept of God is an expression of our understanding of the reality of God at a given time. So are our concepts of the other realities of our faith experience. And, with time and experience, those concepts change and grow toward more comprehensiveness and complexity. We were reminded also in our reflection on that key that there will always be more to the given reality than one's concept of it can completely embrace.

Perhaps here we can make some brief observations/suggestions regarding what happens to faith concepts when they "grow up" toward greater maturity theologically—things to watch for and not be too surprised by as they develop.

A Growing Concept of God

The classic book by J.B. Phillips, *Your God Is Too Small*, addresses the way in which concepts of God can be limited in a way that restricts one's ability to see and experience the reality that God is. Phillips points to images such as "resident policeman," "grand old man," and "managing director" to suggest that these concepts, while helpful as beginning points of thought, are not adequate over time to give expression to the reality of God in a growing covenant relationship.

Concrete images are a natural part of a child's concept of God, but over time there is a maturing that draws that concept in a more comprehensive direction. God becomes not so much a "CEO in the sky" or a "man upstairs" or a "transcendent power on high," but a spirit, a presence, an infusion within life that affects all of its dimensions.

We have noticed how even the concept of God reflected in the biblical testimony undergoes significant transformation and development as the experience behind that testimony matures.

What has happened to your concept of God as that concept has grown up in your faith experience?

A Growing Concept of Jesus

I cannot remember my first impressions of Jesus, but I'm sure he was pretty cool. He could do things other people couldn't do, and he could hold his own against the bad guys of his day—the ones who were always challenging him and his friends for not doing the right things. I do remember how he stood up for people who were being mistreated and couldn't stand up for themselves, and how he helped people who had various ailments and handicaps.

Somewhere along the way, the concept of Jesus as Savior of the world found its way into my experience—Jesus the agent of the reconciliation of humanity to God and to each other from a broken relationship to a "right "one.

Soon, as education began to be a dominant part of my life, both as a consumer of it and as one vocationally involved in it, my concept of Jesus focused on Jesus the teacher—the content and the style of the portraits of him in that role and function were intriguing and memorable.

Needless to say, the concept of Jesus that has evolved in my journey as a follower has included most if not all of the features that have been in the church's teaching throughout its history. But it has also evolved in the direction of seeing him as a personal manifestation of the reality of God—a disclosure of what God has been doing and will continue to do throughout history—and an invitation to participate in that partnership of faith.

How has your concept of Jesus grown up with you in your journey as a follower of him?

A Growing Concept of Salvation

In many parts of the Christian community, a concern for personal salvation is prominent. The focus of evangelical work has often been directly related to "saving souls," "winning the lost," and encouraging people to "accept Jesus as their personal savior." These emphases give prominence to the transformational quality of the faith relationship, and they place much significance on the personal decision at the point of transformation.

For many people, salvation is the "rescue" from the consequences of not being saved—sometimes portrayed as a destiny of punishment in hell. If one is saved, that consequence is avoided. For others, salvation is thought of more in terms of restoration and healing, in the same way that recovery from a disease or addiction is a return to wholeness from a condition of alienation or unhealth. For still others, salvation is a process of growth in which a person moves throughout a lifetime toward the fulfillment of one's potential as a child of God and a partner in the covenant partnership we call faith.

It is not unusual, it seems, for a concept of salvation to start at one place and move to another over the course of the faith journey. The particular orientation of one's specific part of the faith family will have much to do with how salvation is understood, but a general pattern seems to suggest a growth pattern of moving from a rescue from danger to safety to a life process of increasing alignment with a calling to discipleship.

How has your concept of salvation "grown up" in the course of your journey of discipleship?

A Growing Concept of Sin

As a theological concept, sin has had an interesting history and function in the life of the Christian community. A study of its place in Christian theology is well beyond the scope of our reflection here, but it does illustrate the way in which theological concepts can "grow up" theologically from early understandings to ways of thinking that are integrated into the larger framework of faith's reflection.

Most often, it seems, sin is early thought of as misdeeds or patterns of behavior that are contrary to what a life of faith calls one to follow. Certain behaviors and ways of thinking are labeled as sinful and make up a list of sins to be carefully avoided. Drinkin,' dancin,' and lookin' at questionable magazines have at one time made the list.

The origin of this misguided behavior is often traced back to the choice of Adam and Eve to disobey the Lord's rule not to eat from the tree of the knowledge of good and evil in the Garden of Eden (Genesis 3), thus establishing the "original sin" that is passed down through the ages to all people.

Sin as disobedience is easily applicable to lots of areas of life, especially where there are established rules of righteousness and faithfulness—a choice to act outside the parameters of what is acceptable.

A closer look at the Genesis portrayal of that disobedience reveals the reason behind the specific act: a lack of willingness to be content with the creature part of the Creator-creature partnership and a desire to "know as God knows."

A look also at how sin has come to be interpreted theologically reflects an expansion of that concept from a list of "sins" (with a little s) to a condition of "Sin" (with a capital S) that suggests a more comprehensive feature of human experience that can be misaligned with the created purpose of life in covenant relationship. Thinking of sin as alienation or estrangement points to the brokenness of the relationship that faith is, and interpreting it as a "predisposition to act contrary to what faithfulness is" is a broad concept that can cover a multitude of specifics in actual life.

Jesus reflects this broadened concept in his "antinomies" in Matthew's report of the Sermon on the Mount (Matt. 5:17-48). These sayings expand obedience to the Law's true intent by suggesting that obedience is more than keeping the letter of the Law, which can be violated by more subtle expressions that violate its spirit.

A growing-up concept of sin, then, seems to point to an orientation of life that responds in specific ways rather than to a check list of "don'ts."

How, when, and in response to what kinds of circumstances has your concept of sin evolved over the course of your faith journey?

A Growing Concept of Church

"Are you going to church?" "What church do you belong to?" "The library is just past the church on the right." "Will we be having church in light of the prediction of snow and ice?" "I practically grew up in church." "Will you be staying for church after Sunday school today?"

A concept of "church" most likely starts as an image of something physical—a building, a location, a program or worship service that one attends—and these images are certainly a basic part of experiencing "church." Before long, the concept expands to refer to an organization, either on a small scale ("our church") or a large one (the Roman Catholic Church, or the Presbyterian Church). It can be associated primarily with a worship experience, or with a particular fellowship, or with a specific ministry of service. It may start simply, but it gets complex pretty quickly, especially if one is actively involved.

As I am writing this, churches are responding to the challenges of a highly contagious virus that has caused significant alterations in the way churches and other organizations have operated. Schedules have been disrupted, personal contact has been limited, programs have been suspended, and gatherings that once provided intimate fellowship have been shifted to technological substitutes for personal connection. Many congregants have lamented the loss of what church has meant to them, and they have longed for the time when they can "get back to church."

The past couple of years have brought about a forced refinement and growth in the concept of church for many of us. In the absence of many of the structures and institutional frameworks for worship, education, and ministry, many families of faith have discovered new ways of being communities of faith without the traditional structures. A significant part of that discovery has been the realization that "church" is essentially a community of people who share a commitment to a "faith-way" of seeing and responding to the world around them and who can be a community of faith without the traditional frameworks.

In a manner that parallels the Babylonian Exile of Israel/Judah and its effect of enabling the covenant community to rise to new levels of understanding what their covenant meant, contemporary faith families are discovering how to "be church" in challenging times.

This, of course, is a growth pattern that can be observed in people in normal times too, as a concept of church moves toward being more essentially a community rather than an institution, structure, or program. While institutions, structures, and programs are helpful supports for a faith community's life, the theological growth of a concept of church seems to move in the direction of community.

Can you recall the "growth steps" in your concept of church? What were some of the experiences and influences that helped shape your understanding of church from your earliest impressions to where that understanding is now?

Other Theological Concepts That "Grow Up"

We could add other concepts to our list, for there are many that are a part of our religious thinking (prayer, love, hope, heaven, eternal life) that can be observed to evolve over the course of the pilgrimage

Our observations here are intended to suggest a couple of important things for everyday theologians. One, the features of the faith experience will always be seen through the lens of our concepts of those realities, and our concepts will always have the possibility of moving in the direction of the realities themselves. Two, remember that we not only engage in that process ourselves, but we also participate in that growth process for others as companions and coaches for one another as we move along the journey. As we grow in our own thinking, we model and assist others in theirs.

Conclusion

Theology as a Pilgrimage Toward Community

Our conversation as everyday theologians began with the assumption that every person of faith is by definition a theologian. Employing St. Anselm's definition of theology as "faith seeking understanding," we started with another assumption that faith, especially in the covenant testimony of the Bible and subsequent history, is essentially a relational term—pointing to the inherent connection between what is experienced as the divine mystery and what is experienced in human life.

These two assumptions underscore the basic point that faith is not primarily a body of beliefs and ideas to embrace and defend, but a relationship to participate in and to grow within.

Theology as "faith seeking understanding," then, is a pilgrimage toward broader and deeper understanding of that relationship and participation in a community of fellow pilgrims to help and be helped by each other.

Reflecting on the journey brought us to consider some "conceptual keys" that can serve to unlock the doors to some of the rooms of the theological house, and to some of the outer porches that enable us to look beyond the walls of our own house to the dwelling places of other faiths.

To recap with a quick summary of our keys, they have invited us to…

1. Consider the relation of faith as a relationship and theology as the work of understanding and interpreting that relationship.
2. Distinguish between the relationship itself and the beliefs that accompany that relationship and that inevitably grow and change as the relationship matures.
3. Recognize and remain aware of the partiality of our own thinking in our quest for understanding, claiming enough but not too much for the truth as we see it at a given time.
4. Understand with as much care and honesty as possible the sources of guidance in our quest for understanding—the Bible, church tradition, and our personal experience.
5. Cultivate discernment for use in the marketplace of religious guidance, to choose a "theological diet" that is healthy and nutritious for this dimension of our lives.
6. Understand the different "levels of truth" in religious literature and to discern what level is operative and being affirmed in a given part of the testimony.

7. Understand the partnership of religious thinking and scientific thinking in living responsibly and faithfully in our world—not allowing these two essential ways of relating to our world to become adversaries and competitors for our commitment.
8. Understand the relation of faith and history in a faith tradition that is rooted in history, mediated through history, and lived in history in real time with a vision of history's direction.
9. Understand and embrace in ourselves and others the level of personal and religious maturity that is the context of our and their search for understanding.
10. Respond faithfully to an increasing awareness of the many other faith traditions in the human family.

Using these keys should keep us busy for a while, unlocking the interior doors of our faith to reveal deeper insights waiting to be found. Some of them also unlock the doors to outer porches that offer a view toward other theological houses, whose spiritual insights are waiting to be shared.

Let's leave with some questions that look forward: Where do we go from here? What is the trajectory of this pilgrimage of our faith seeking understanding? Toward what goal can the focus of everyday theologians be directed to stay on the path of faith seeking understanding?

I want to suggest here for our ongoing consideration that the trajectory of the theological quest is toward a theology of community. To see faith as essentially a relationship is to align with the core of the biblical testimony of covenant faith and to embrace its vision of faithful living as a pilgrimage toward community.

Community seems to be the natural consequence of faithful relationship, especially when it is characterized by honesty, hospitality, intellectual and theological humility, and respect for and a willingness to engage the insights of one another. When people "think about their own thinking" and share the fruits of that thinking with one another, a community develops that is of a different character from the other (perfectly valid and appropriate) communities that fill our lives.

A community of everyday theologians on a pilgrimage together seems to be the goal of the covenant calling. Each of our keys has reflected this relational feature, suggesting that the purpose of theological thinking is to enrich relationships both on a personal and a communal level.

Among the several uses of the image of the kingdom of God in the gospels is Jesus' word to those he had called to be the forerunners of today's everyday theologians: "The kingdom of God is among/within you" (Luke 17:21). Those who are the theological heirs of that assertion are the community that embodies the Kingdom in every generation.

So, maybe the "master key" for our set of more particular keys is this thought:

Theology = Faith Seeking Understanding = A Pilgrimage Toward Community

Yes, you are a theologian—one of the most important kind. Perhaps this is at least part of the meaning of Jesus' affirmation to Simon Peter, who had just offered his own profession of faith, that he would build his community of followers (the church) on the foundation of that faith: "[And] I will give you the keys of the kingdom of heaven, and whatever you bind on earth will be bound in heaven, and whatever you loose on earth will be loosed in heaven" (Matt. 16:19).

Hang onto your keys. They will be useful on the pilgrimage.

9 781635 281798